CSR, Sustainability, Ethics & Governance

Series editors

More information about this series at http://www.springer.com/series/11565

Saumitra N. Bhaduri · Ekta Selarka

Corporate Governance and Corporate Social Responsibility of Indian Companies

Springer

Saumitra N. Bhaduri
Madras School of Economics
Chennai, Tamil Nadu
India

Ekta Selarka
Madras School of Economics
Chennai, Tamil Nadu
India

ISSN 2196-7075 ISSN 2196-7083 (electronic)
CSR, Sustainability, Ethics & Governance
ISBN 978-981-10-0924-2 ISBN 978-981-10-0925-9 (eBook)
DOI 10.1007/978-981-10-0925-9

Library of Congress Control Number: 2016936569

Printed on acid-free paper

This Springer imprint is published by Springer Nature
The registered company is Springer Science+Business Media Singapore Pte Ltd.

Acknowledgments

We gratefully acknowledge the project grant from the Indian Council of Social Science Research to support this study. Research assistance from Dr. A. Balasubramanian is highly appreciated. We also acknowledge the assistance provided by Mr. Bishu Giri and Mr. Ranveer Sengupta during the process of data collection.

Also, this project would not have been possible without the institutional support from Professors. K.R. Shanmugam and Sunder Ramaswamy and the administrative team at the Madras School of Economics.

In addition, we sincerely acknowledge the inputs from the members of ICSSR Advisory Committee—Professors Madheswaran, Hemnath Rao and Krishna Prasanna. We gratefully appreciate their efforts and time in reading our chapters and providing valuable inputs. We are also thankful to the referees at the Springer to provide bird's eye view and inputs that shaped this manuscript further.

Finally, we thank our families for their love and support. Ekta Selarka specifically acknowledges Devang for his continuous encouragement & support and Reva for her endless patience during all phases of this project.

Saumitra N. Bhaduri
Ekta Selarka

Contents

About the Authors

Saumitra N. Bhaduri obtained a Master's degree in Econometrics from Calcutta University and a Ph.D. in Financial Economics from the Indira Gandhi Institute of Development Research (IGIDR), Mumbai, India. He is currently Professor at the Madras School of Economics (MSE), Chennai, India, and regularly offers courses in financial economics and econometrics, and advanced quantitative techniques. He previously worked at the financial services division of the General Electric (GE) company and has held a number of quantitative analyst positions in the various finance services of the company. He has also founded and headed the GE–MSE Decision Sciences Laboratory, which is responsible for developing state-of-the-art research output for GE. He has published several research articles in various international journals.

Ekta Selarka obtained a Bachelor's degree in Electrical Engineering from Bhilai Institute of Technology, Bhilai, India, and a Ph.D. in Economics from Indira Gandhi Institute of Development Research (IGIDR), Mumbai. She is currently a faculty at the Madras School of Economics (MSE), Chennai, where she offers courses in financial economics, derivatives, market microstructure and financial programming using SAS, VBA and Matlab. Prior to joining MSE she worked as a research economist at IGIDR and as a risk analyst with GE Capital. Her research interests include corporate governance, ownership structure, capital market development and corporate performance. She has published in international journals such as *Journal of Corporate Finance*, and *Emerging Markets Trade and Finance*. She has received prestigious research grants from Indian Council of Social Science and Research (ICSSR) and UK-India Education and Research Initiative (UKIERI) through collaborations with researchers in India as well as abroad.

Executive Summary

This study aims to investigate the interaction between Corporate Governance and Corporate Social Responsibility (CSR) activities undertaken by Indian corporate. We find by reviewing the available literature that there is no single theoretical background which couples the CSR and the corporate governance at the firm level together and therefore to build a research framework, various theories from transaction cost economics and organization behaviour are needed to be explored.

Our study provides an extensive literature survey describing the interaction between CSR and corporate governance deriving from an academic literature as well as survey reports across the world. The interdisciplinary nature of our research framework that cuts across behaviour economics and management science to understand the interaction between CSR and corporate governance yields a comprehensive literature review which to best of our knowledge is missing. From the review of literature, we propose our empirical analysis to build on competing hypotheses as: (1) On the one hand, CSR can be thought of an extended model of "Corporate Governance" which implies inclusion of CSR into the check box of "Good" corporate governance practices that will complement the effect of good corporate governance. (2) On the other hand, the abuse of CSR may also result by just opening another way of expropriation of small investors by dominant promoters and large shareholders. This is an empirical question and provides implications for the two mechanisms that have profound impact on firm's objective function.

The empirical framework developed to investigate the impact of governance practices on corporate social responsibility accounts for the sample selection bias and measurement error which is pervasive in most of the existing studies on CSR and corporate governance. Apart from its contribution through a robust empirical framework to analyse the interaction between the corporate governance and CSR, data per se also adds a lot of value to our study. Unlike many studies which utilizes the secondary data provided by Karmayog, Forbes, CSR Identity, etc. we have meticulously hand-picked the data by carefully scrutinizing the publicly available information for each of the companies in our sample. This process has yielded a unique 3-year panel data for large 500 firms with detailed information on CSR activities across all the possible avenues. We believe that this unique dataset can be utilized further to support other future researches on CSR. We predict CSR score for every company in our sample using the distribution obtained from our empirical model which is further validated across different categories of CSR spending—no CSR, low CSR, medium CSR and high CSR. We propose that this score can be used as an important tool to predict the probability of a firm being classified in a particular range of CSR. We also validate this scoring methodology for a random set of companies selected out of our existing sample. This ensures the applicability of our methodology to predict the likelihood of undertaking CSR activity by a firm which can be used by policy makers as well as researchers in future.

Our first estimation methodology controls for the sample selection as in absence of regulatory compliance, many of the firms do not report amount spent on CSR and report disclosure of CSR activities instead.

We find that firms which are older, larger and pay dividend are more likely to undertake the CSR activities. We also find significant positive relationship between CSR and proportion of controlling shareholders which implies that founding families or government are driven by strategic decision of investing into CSR-related activities. This is also in line with the positive relationship between insiders' control over board and CSR. In contrast, fraction of independent directors does not affect the CSR even though our univariate analysis suggests that firms with higher proportion of independent directors spend more on CSR activities.

To our surprise, profitability does not have any significant relationship with CSR activities. This questions the recent mandate of diverting 2 % of the profit towards CSR activities in the Companies Act 2013. It is worth noting that some of the puzzling results presented in this section could be due to the unobservable nature of our attributes such as corporate governance along with the inaccurate measurement of the proxies to capture these attributes. We attempt to address some of these challenges in the following chapter by developing a structural equation model.

Further, the results are robust to the out of sample validation. We also develop a robust methodology to predict the propensity of CSR activities that are likely to be undertaken by the firms based on four categories—no, low, medium and high CSR—respectively. This method is tested and validated for a random sample of 50 companies that are not part of our sample.

We further present the structural equation model that address two critical issues related to the unobservability of the attributes derived from various theoretical constructs and potential measurement errors. Further the proposed model also incorporates the possibility of cross-correlations across the unobservable factors. The results show that all the four specified attributes—structure, financial constraint, corporate governance and duality—significantly influence the CSR spending of large Indian firms. More specifically, we find evidence that poor corporate governance coupled with insider control over the board tend to explain the variation in CSR activities across firms. The other conventional factors such as age, size and financial viability of a firm also contribute to the CSR spending by these firms.

Finally, we test whether firms by engaging into socially responsible activities gain (or lose) returns in excess of the market in the structural equation framework that we develop to account for unobservability of the attributes and measurement errors. We find that market does not differentiate whether the firm undertakes CSR activities. In addition, the financial constraint attribute of the firm significantly and positively affects the excess returns, while poor corporate governance does not impact on the excess returns. This finding implies that the conventional factors such as dividend payout, profitability and leverage matter more to the investors. This in turn supports the stakeholder approach rather than the shareholder value maximization approach of analysing CSR.

Chapter 1
Corporate Governance and Corporate Social Responsibility—Introduction

1.1 Introduction

Corporate governance reform has emerged as a critical business and economic issue at the global level followed by a number of high profile corporate failures. At the same time, as early as 2005, the international economic press acknowledged the growth of Corporate Social Responsibility (CSR) initiatives of the world organisations. The Economist mentioned:

> Today all companies, but especially the big ones, are enjoined from every side to worry less about profits and to be socially responsible instead. Surprisingly, perhaps, these demands have elicited a willing, not to say avid, response in enlightened boardrooms everywhere: companies at every opportunity now pay elaborate obeisance to the principle of CSR. They have CSR officers, CSR consultants, CSR departments, and CSR initiatives coming out of their ears. (The Economist, 22 January 2005, p. 11)

The above quote reflects the current wisdom regarding the insufficient commitment of organizations about making profits for their shareholders by engaging themselves in "pernicious benevolence" and being philanthropic at the cost of shareholder's money. This also resonates with the famous dictum by Milton Friedman of the 1970s that:

> …there is one and only one social responsibility of business–to use it resources and engage in activities designed to increase its profits so long as it stays within the rules of the game, which is to say, engages in open and free competition without deception or fraud. (The New York Times, September 13, 1970)

Against this backdrop, there has been a conscious attempt during the early 21st century to reform the corporate governance policies to rationalize the growing CSR activities across international, region and national fronts. The notion of CSR grew up from being merely philanthropic to an appendix of the core business strategy. At the international level CSR was included in company level initiatives, as well as in the multi-stakeholder initiatives at national and international levels such as the UN global compact. The concept of practicing CSR was adopted in the UK which was one of the traditional Anglo-American model of corporate

S.N. Bhaduri and E. Selarka, *Corporate Governance and Corporate Social Responsibility of Indian Companies*, CSR, Sustainability, Ethics & Governance,
DOI 10.1007/978-981-10-0925-9_1

responsibility and governance by reorienting its system of corporate law around the objective of 'enlightened shareholder value'. This reform formally makes the law of directors' duties and corporate reporting ostensibly more stakeholder inclusive.

Recent literature on corporate governance has redefined the corporate governance definition as a system of mechanisms—market oriented and institutional—that benefits all the constituents of society. This definition still builds on the conventional shareholder value maximization while considering the benefits accruing to all the stakeholders. While many regulatory efforts have been initiated to identify and codify good governance practices to rebuild public and market trust, there are a parallel number of efforts to broaden the social and environmental boundaries of corporate governance. The UN Global Compact's 2004 report, "Who Cares Wins," which looks at the social, environmental and governance issues that can have a material impact on corporate financial performance, is one of many recent reports investigating the links between social, environmental and governance practices as follows:

> In a more globalized, interconnected and competitive world, the way that environmental, social and corporate governance issues are managed is part of companies' overall management quality needed to compete successfully. Companies that perform better with regard to these issues can increase shareholder value by, for example, properly managing risks, anticipating regulatory action or accessing new markets while at the same time contributing to the sustainable development of the societies in which they operate. Moreover these issues can have a strong impact on reputation and brands, an increasingly important part of company value.

Therefore, regardless of the type of organizational structure, effective corporate governance should ensure an efficient utilization of all available resources including the resources being utilized for CSR. An ideal system of corporate governance should avoid any sub-optimal value maximization exercise stemming from "pernicious benevolence" that might arise due to poor corporate governance characteristics. Specifically, while an increase in CSR expenditure may be consistent with firm value maximization if it is a response to changes in stakeholders' preferences, we argue that a firm's insiders (managers and large block holders) may seek to over-invest in CSR for their private benefit to the extent that doing so improves their reputations as good global citizens. We test this hypothesis by investigating the relation between firms' CSR spending and their corporate governance practices. On one hand this is the classical agency problem, on the other hand, CSR can be thought of an extended model of corporate governance which facilitates regulatory monitoring and a threat of shareholder activism to discipline entrenched insiders. This kind of framework requires analysis of interaction between the two.

By focusing on corporate governance practices, we essentially focus whether CSR gives rise to the risk of expropriation by the controlling shareholders. This requires formal analysis of business ethics as perceived by the board members.

More recently, business and academic researchers have shown increasing interests in the CSR. The theme of environmental and social responsibility appears in a number of political and legal documents and is gaining ever-greater importance at the international level. Today, corporate leaders face a dynamic and challenging task in combining societal ethical standards to their business practices. This is also corroborated by the fact that the social responsibility was ranked as second most important business challenges for companies in a survey of 750 Chief Executive Officers conducted by the Financial Times and Price Waterhouse Coopers (Hopkins 2000). Therefore, companies especially those operating in global markets, are increasingly required to balance the social, economic and environmental components of their business, while building shareholder value (Maignan and Ralston 2002).

1.2 Globalisation, Corporate Governance and Social Responsibility

An understanding of the strengths and weaknesses of competitive markets suggests a role for CSR programs. Competitive markets are strong—produce efficient outcomes—when private and social costs and benefits are the same. In this case what is most profitable to the corporation is also best for society. Conflicts between corporations and society over environmental issues almost always derive from private-social cost differences associated with pollution, the latter being the classic example of such differences. Some of the costs of an activity are externalized to the population as a whole through the spread of pollutants. Global warming, acid rain and pollution in cities are all examples of social costs exceeding private and consequent conflicts between corporate actors and society. Deforestation is another source of environmental conflict, again driven by differences in costs and benefits (Heal 2005).

The financial sector has also been accused of its share of unfair practices, usually involving discriminating against retail market participants either through insider trading, through unfair allocations at IPOs or through unfair allocations to "related parties", or involving conflicts of interest at intermediaries.

In the literature as well as in practice, CSR has played a major role in environmental conflicts. Companies like British Petroleum (BP) provides a case by taking a stand on climate change and imposing a firm-wide cap on greenhouse gas emissions and began a corporate emissions trading system[1] viewed from an economic perspective, what BP has done is to acknowledge that its operating costs—private costs—are less than the social costs of its activities, and take measures to bring the two into line. Most of these companies which came under the radar of this conflict with society formulated their own solutions. A well-executed CSR program not only will remove the conflict between a corporation and society, but will also document convincingly, perhaps through outside audits, that this has been done.

[1]Harvard Business School case on Global Climate Change and BP Amoco (2000).

One can also argue that another source of corporate-societal conflict making headlines in recent years relates to the wages paid by rich-country firms in poor countries (distributional conflicts across global regions). Does that mean the BPOs get negative marking in CSR?

1.3 The Competitive Advantage and Corporate Social Responsibility

Porter and Kramer (2006) argue that CSR can be much more than a cost, a constraint, or a charitable deed it can be a source of opportunity, innovation and competitive advantage. Stakeholder Theory of corporate governance brings the role of society formally into firm's value maximization objective function by arguing that managers should make decisions so as to take account of the interests of all stakeholders in a firm (including not only financial claimants, but also employees, customers, communities, governmental official and environment). This theory essentially extends the objective function of a firm by suggesting that the choice of value maximization as the corporate scorecard must be complemented by a corporate vision, strategy and tactics that unite participants in the organization in its struggle for dominance in its competitive arena (Jensen 2001). Undertaking of socially responsible activities is one way the governments and leaders have argued to implement what is called the corporate philanthropy. This again provides us a strong background to conduct analysis of interaction between CSR and Corporate governance at the firm level.

Building on the corporate responsibility is the concept of Triple Bottom Line (TBL) to include the CSR into business practice by recognizing the objectives of a corporate to maximize Economic, Social and Environmental performance. The TBL provides a standardization of corporate statements about firm's social, environmental and economic performance (CPA, Australia 2004). This method has become the standard accounting practice volunteered across a large number of firms in developed countries.

1.4 Varying Definitions of CSR

In most of the regulations and initiatives taken by corporations, CSR is defined in terms of philanthropic activities. Yet the definitions provided by regulators across the globe vary. European Union defines CSR as a program in which companies decide voluntarily to contribute to a better society and a cleaner environment (Beltratti 2004). International Labor Organization discussion paper states that CSR is concerned with treating stakeholders of the firm ethically or in a responsible manner (Hopkins 2007). The OECD guidelines suggest that the common aim of the governments adhering to the guidelines of Corporate Social Responsibility is to encourage the positive contributions that multinational enterprises can make to economic, environmental and social progress and to minimize the difficulties to which their various operations may give rise (OECD 2001). This is clearly seeing CSR as a move to increase the social value added by corporate activity. Beltratti (2004) makes an interesting comment that CSR is an attempt to escape profit maximization in the recognition that agency problems and incomplete contracts undermine the basic idea of shareholders supremacy. This comes close to the tradition established by Ronald Coase in his paper "The Problem of Social Cost."

1.5 Corporate Governance and Corporate Social Responsibility—Indian Perspective

Consistent with the global trends, India has also witnessed a surge in the CSR reforms in recent times. However, it is important to note the concept of CSR is not new to India as business groups like Tata and Birla have been imbibing the case for social good in their operations for decades long before CSR become a popular cause.

The new Companies Act 2013 formally specifies the CSR activities and implementation through board committees. Indeed India has become the first country to make CSR mandatory through following:

1. The new Companies Act 2013 mandates 2 % of profit to be spent on CSR. This is applicable on the companies with more than Rs. 500 crore net worth. However, the Companies Act 2013 does not define the CSR but provides the list of activities that can be included by companies in their CSR activities.
2. Along with other committees, CSR committee should be formed and chaired by an Independent Director. In addition, the Companies Act 2013 also revises the definition of independent director and the board independence requirement.
3. SEBI's mandate for listed companies, starting with the top 100 firms, to describe measures taken by them along the key principles enunciated in the 'National voluntary guidelines on social, environmental and economic responsibilities of business,' framed by the Ministry of Corporate Affairs (MCA).

Therefore, the current effort to blend the corporate governance with CSR enforced through regulation provides a unique opportunity for a natural experiment to analyze the interaction between quality of governance and its effect of CSR activities undertaken by firms in India. However, it is important to note that unlike developed countries, India has a specific corporate governance problem of disciplining dominant shareholders who are in control of the management and most of the times serve on the board because of concentrated nature of their ownership, the fiduciary duties of board in general can be questioned. Existing research on India supports the evidence that large outside shareholders and mergers and acquisitions are not quite effective as corporate governance mechanisms. In such a scenario, mandating CSR may lead to curb the expropriation activities and increased reputational effects that would force managers to use resources efficiently and constraint private benefits of control.

1.6 Objective of the Study

This study builds on an enhanced framework (Fig. 1.1) of the conventional theory of value maximization which not only focuses on shareholder value maximization but also incorporates social welfare, and the accountability of managers and directors to the stakeholders. We conduct a comparative analysis of various organisational structures such as public sector enterprises, private sector firms and banking companies to understand and identify CSR activities. We quantify CSR activities of largest 500 Indian companies using both qualitative and quantitative information on CSR activities. This meticulous collection of information lends a strong reliability to our analysis which is usually missing in many of the existing studies. We also collect data on corporate governance characteristics such as—board size, composition, entrenchment structure, independence, and ownership. These variables are widely used in the corporate governance theory and practice to describe the quality of corporate governance practices at the firm level.

Our study intends to address some of the most fundamental issues in the interaction between CSR and corporate governance and also considers the best approach to the measurement of CSR. The purpose of this study is to probe the interaction of CSR and corporate governance to understand the impact of firm level governance practices in determining the CSR related activities.

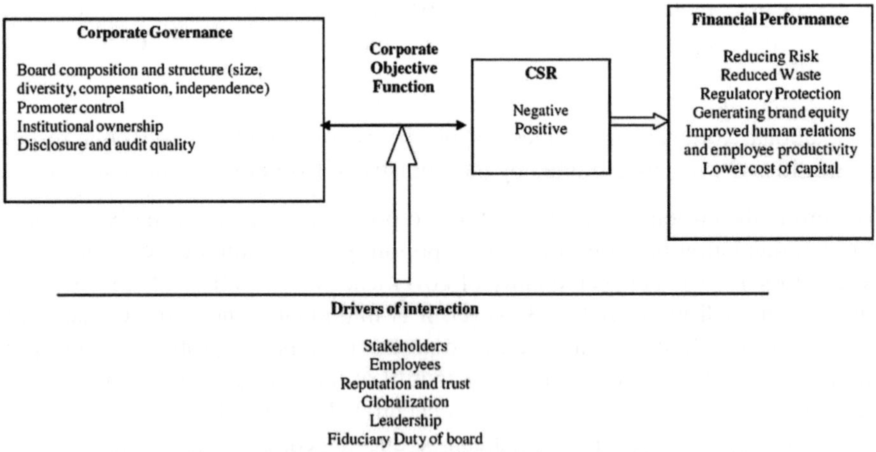

Fig. 1.1 Framework for the interaction between CSR and CG

Our study also contributes to the literature that looks at the link between the corporate governance and stakeholders' interest when the society as a whole is the stakeholder. The research on explicit formalization of the link between corporate governance and stakeholders' interests is still evolving. Pagano and Volpin (2005) analyze the relationship between managers, shareholders, and workers. Their focus is on how long-term contracts and high wages, which benefit employees (stakeholders), can protect managers against hostile takeovers. In another study, Cespa and Cestone (2007) investigate the conflicts of interest that might arise between managers, shareholders, and other stakeholders in the case where managers rather than firms can commit to CSR, and stakeholders other than shareholders can influence the manager's replacement. In our study, we focus directly on the principal-agent problem between insides and outside shareholders.

1.7 Measurement of Corporate Governance

Measuring corporate governance is however more difficult since governance encompasses a large number of mechanisms. Existing evidence on effectiveness of corporate governance mechanisms in Indian corporate mostly concentrated on large shareholders and concentration of ownership in the hands of family or group business. However, there are many more like board independence, board size, independent audit committees, existence of remuneration committees, disclosure, capital structure, etc. For the purpose of this study we propose to focus on board structure, composition and independence. As the new Companies Act directly focus on the board structure and composition/independence, direct analysis of board effectiveness is required.

In addition to, despite the surge in research on corporate governance in emerging markets, we still know little about firms' actual corporate governance practices. In this study we provide a detailed, descriptive account of the governance practices of firms in an important emerging market in India. This study allows us to provide a rich picture of the governance practices of Indian boards directly related to CSR activities.

1.8 Data Sources and Empirical Methodology

The secondary data on other corporate governance variables such as ownership structure, board composition are collected from the Prowess database which is being maintained by the Centre for Monitoring Indian Economy. Prowess is one of the largest databases of listed companies which compile historical information from annual reports and corporate governance reports. This database is being used by national as well as international scholars to conduct firm and industry level studies. We source the financial, industry specific and corporate governance information on sample companies from Prowess. We augment data sourced from Prowess with the management and director's report for the sample companies to locate information on management's interest in CSR.

We develop a framework that accounts for the sample selection bias that stems from non-disclosure of actual expenditure on CSR activities that may not necessary indicate absence of CSR initiative by a company. This framework helps us to construct propensity of CSR as a categorical variable that captures four categories of CSR—No, Low, Medium and High levels of CSR—respectively. Further, we use this construct to investigate the impact of corporate governance structures on CSR activities undertaken by our sample firms.

In addition, we explain and address some of the puzzling results that we find by employing an advanced method of structural equation modelling. This technique accounts for the unobservability of the theoretical constructs and measurement errors in various proxies.

1.9 Contribution and Organisation of the Study

We propose to utilize the specific characteristics of Indian corporate governance practices to investigate whether the "effective" corporate governance complements or substitutes the CSR activities. The contribution of our study is three-fold:

1. Our study provides an extensive literature survey describing the interaction between CSR and corporate governance deriving from an academic literature as well as survey reports across the world. The interdisciplinary nature of our research framework that cuts across behaviour economics and management science to understand the interaction between CSR and corporate governance yields a comprehensive literature review which to best of our knowledge is missing. Therefore, this can be utilized to build research questions in future as well.
2. The empirical framework developed to investigate the impact of governance practices on corporate social responsibility accounts for the sample selection bias and measurement error which is pervasive in most of the existing studies on CSR and corporate governance.
3 Apart from its contribution through a robust empirical framework to analyze the interaction between the corporate governance and CSR, data per se also adds a lot of value to our study. Unlike many studies which utilizes the secondary data provided by Karmayogi, Forbes, CSR Identity etc., we have meticulously hand-picked the data by carefully scrutinizing the publicly available information for each of the companies in our sample. This process has yielded a unique three year panel data for large 500 firms with detailed information on CSR activities across all the possible avenues. We believe that this unique dataset can be utilized further to support other future researches on CSR.

4. We predict CSR score for every company in our sample using the distribution obtained from our empirical model which is further validated across different categories of CSR spending namely—No CSR, Low CSR, Medium CSR and High CSR respectively. We propose that this score can be used as an important tool to predict the probability of a firm being classified in a particular range of CSR. We also validate this scoring methodology for a random set of companies selected out of our existing sample. This ensures the applicability of our methodology to predict the likelihood of undertaking CSR activity by a firm which can be used by policy makers as well as researchers in future.

This study is organized as follows. Chapter 2 presents the evolution of CSR and related theories that would help us to quantify CSR variables. This chapter also presents the consumer and management based surveys around the world to draw upon the business strategies evolved around the CSR in developed as well as developing and emerging countries. Chapter 3 presents the global guidelines and best practices for corporations engaging into the CSR related activities. Chapter 4 presents the guidelines and best practices adopted in India. Chapter 5 provides an overview of corporate governance theories and mechanisms that help us to quantify proxies to capture corporate governance structures in India. Chapter 6 presents the empirical literature and builds on the limitation of current studies. The chapter also presents our unique dataset and the preliminary analysis of the data. Specifically we present our observations on evolving CSR trends in large 500 companies listed on Bombay Stock Exchange. Chapter 7 presents the empirical modelling to analyse the relationship between corporate governance and CSR. Finally, Chap. 8 addresses the limitations of the existing empirical methodology through structural equation modelling and revisits our research question to find robust results on the underlying research question.

References

Beltratti A (2004) The complementarity between corporate governance and corporate social responsibility, Bocconi University
Cespa G, Cestone G (2007) Corporate social responsibility and managerial entrenchment. J Econ Manag Strategy 16(3):741–771
Heal G (2005) Corporate social responsibility: an economic and financial framework. Geneva Pap 30(3):387–409
Hopkins M (2000) The measurement of corporate social responsibility' MHC International Limited News Nov 2000
Hopkins M (2007) Corporate social responsibility and international development: Is business the solution? London: Earthscan
Jensen MC (2001) Value maximization, stakeholder theory, and the corporate objective function. J Appl Corp Finance 14(3):8–21
Maignan I , Ralston D (2002) Corporate social responsibility in Europe and the U.S.: Insights from Businesses' Self-Presentations. J Int B Stud, 33:497–514
Organization for Economic Co-operation and Development (OECD) (2001) Corporate responsibility: private initiatives and public goals. OECD, Paris

Pagano M, Volpin PF (2005) The political economy of corporate governance. Am Econ Rev, 1005–1030

Porter ME , Kramer MR (2006) Strategy and Society: The Link between Competitive Advantage and Corporate Social Responsibility. Harvard Business Review 84(12)

Reinhardt FL (2000) Global climate change and BP Amoco. Harvard Business School Case Study, N9-700-106

Chapter 2
Corporate Social Responsibility Around the World—An Overview of Theoretical Framework, and Evolution

2.1 Introduction

The objective of this chapter is to highlight the evolution of the concept of the corporate social responsibility around the world. Specifically, we focus on theoretical framework underpinning the corporate social responsibility. We also review various definitions highlighting some of the most widely used definitions which are exhaustive in nature. We conclude the chapter by providing a summary of various surveys conducted across the world by various agencies to understand the nature of CSR spending from differing perspectives of employees, consumers and management.

Corporate social responsibility has changed the role of doing business in the society, from simple exhortation of no social duties for business to the understanding of being socially responsible. Around the globe, various scholars, reporting agencies and institutions have already started to explore the multiple aspects of this concept both theoretically and empirically. Formalising corporate social responsibility for a corporation builds on the perspective of multi-faceted stakeholders. The basic understanding of widening the responsibility of corporate from shareholder perspective to its all stakeholder approach leads business to play different roles for its different players. However, the challenge is of providing a universally accepted definition of activities to be described as socially responsible behaviour.

In simple terms CSR can be understood from the three words the phrase contains: "Corporate" which covers the large spectrum of businesses, "Social" refers to the local community with which they interact and finally by incorporating "Responsibilities" that are intrinsic on both sides of these relationships. Hence, CSR is nothing but corporate in its widest sense and on many levels, to include all stakeholders and constituent groups that maintain an ongoing interest in the organization's operations along with the society within which it operates.

S.N. Bhaduri and E. Selarka, *Corporate Governance and Corporate Social Responsibility of Indian Companies*, CSR, Sustainability, Ethics & Governance,
DOI 10.1007/978-981-10-0925-9_2

2.2 Origin and Evolution of Corporate Social Responsibility

Though the roots of the concept of corporate social responsibility have a long and evolving history, it is mostly a product of the twentieth century, especially from the early 1920s up to the present time. In spite of its recent growth and popularity, one can trace for centuries evidence of the business community's concern for society. Over past six decades it has been discussed in the literature (Bowen 1953) that corporate do have a social responsibility, in the context of widening the accountability of firms performance.

In recent decades, CSR as a concept, has been the focus of many deliberations and research. It has grown in importance both academically as well as in the business sense. It captures a spectrum of values and criteria for measuring a company's contribution to social development.

The central theme of the concept of corporate social responsibility is that the social responsibilities are the social forces operating in every society making corporates to act in a certain way. This is true regardless of whether it is a capitalist or a socialist society as the social forces are always there. These may not allow the business to deviate from the course of social responsibility. These forces may wipe out all such enterprises which prove contrary to social interests. The activities of a corporation impact upon the external environment and that therefore such an organization should be accountable to a wider audience than simply its shareholders.

The core perception of business has some social responsibilities has emerged for the past three hundred years ago from a renowned Scottish philosopher and economist, Adam Smith, in The Wealth of Nations. He describes the support for market interactions that are freely participated in by individuals and organizations, saying that they could serve the needs of the society. Further, people engage in commerce or business out of selfish (Invisible Hand) reasons, or for their personal benefits, but in one way or other this would also benefit the society as a whole with positive or negative externalities. This implies that the corporations should also enhance the welfare of the society by protecting and nurturing the interests of the society. Recently, scholars like Brown and Forster (2013) have further substantiated the Smith's idea of corporate social responsibility.

The concept of business ethics or corporate philanthropy has its roots way back in 1920s through concepts of public service (Smith 1759) and trusteeship (Clark 1939). Bowen (1953) has further formally introduced the concept of Businessmen's social responsibilities which provided the much needed foundation for the development of the modern concept of CSR. By bringing in the concept of "stewardship", Friedman (1970) has further enhanced the Smith's view on CSR.

Carroll (1979, 1999a, b) further formalized Bowen's arguments to build models on the escalating concept of CSR. In 1980s the concept of CSR further transcends to a broader concept of corporate social responsiveness and corporate citizenship which further translates to Corporate Social Performance (CSP), which has been

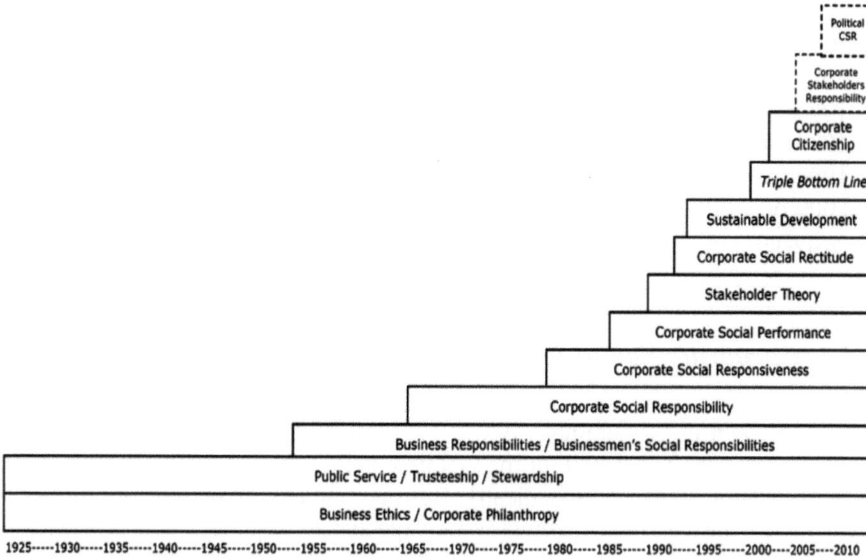

Fig. 2.1 Escalating concept of corporate social responsibility. *Source* Adopted from Mohan (2003) and Gond and Moon (2011)

widely studied by many authors. The interrelationship between the CSP and firm performance and profitability was also extensively explored by many authors such as Cochran and Wood (1984), Aupperle et al. (1985), Waddock and Graves (1997).

Since 1980s the concept of the CSR has evolved in terms of the Stakeholder theory (Freeman 1984) which formed the base for understanding the relationship between CSR and Sustainable Development during 1990s. Around this time, nations around the world started framing guidelines, regulations and principles for adopting CSR as a best practice by corporations. This, further brought a new dimension called the Triple Bottom Line during 2000s which has initiated the modern concepts of CSR as Corporate Citizenship, Corporate Stakeholder Responsibility and Political CSR. Mohan (2003) and Gond and Moon (2011) have summarized the escalating concept of CSR since 1920s, which depicts the roadmap of the evolution of the concept of the CSR till date. Figure 2.1 graphically presents the escalating concept of CSR following the works of Mohan (2003) and Gond and Moon (2011).

2.3 Concept of Corporate Social Responsibility: Timeline

Following section summarizes the historical evolution of the concept CSR into six phases from 1950s to after 2000 respectively. We also elaborate on origin and development of the concept of CSR in each of these phases.

The aforementioned six phases are as follows:

1950–1960s—Period of Introduction of CSR in the academic arena and corporate philanthropy as CSR

1970s—Period of rapid growth in the concept of CSR

1980s—Period of Stakeholder Theory and Business Ethics

1990s—Period of CSR Practicing by Corporate

2000 onwards—Period of empirical works to investigate the determinants and consequences of CSR on corporate strategy

2.3.1 Corporate Social Responsibility in—1950s

Howard Bowen in his seminal work in 1953 titled as "Social Responsibilities of the Businessman" introduced for the first time the concept of Social Responsibility in the academic research. Specifically, Bowen enquired "What responsibilities to society may businessmen reasonably be expected to assume?" and provided the initial definition of the social responsibility as "… it refers to the obligations of businessmen to pursue those policies, to make those decisions, or to follow those lines of action which are desirable in terms of the objectives and values of our society". Bowen's (1953) work proceeded from the belief that the several hundred largest businesses at the time were vital centers of power and decision making and that the actions of these firms touched the lives of citizens in many ways as observed by Carroll (2006).

Subsequently, another influential contribution to the early definitions of social responsibility was made by Frederick (1960). Frederick (1960) specifies that "social responsibility [in the final analysis] implies a public posture toward society's economic and human resources and a willingness to see that those resources are utilized for broad social ends and not simply for the narrowly circumscribed interests of private persons and firm". Frederick (1950) points out three core ideas of trusteeship and corporate philanthropy:

1. Corporate managers as public trustees,
2. Balance of competing claims to corporate resources and,
3. The acceptance of philanthropy as a manifestation of business support of good causes.

Murphy (1978) has also classified the growth of CSR in four eras in which he has described the 1950s as the 'philanthropic' era during which companies primarily donated to charities.

2.3.2 Corporate Social Responsibility as Philanthropy in 1960s

The decade of the 1960s marked as a period of momentous growth in the attempts to formalize the definition of Corporate Social Responsibility. However, philanthropy continued as the most noticeable manifestation of CSR during the 1960s.

Davis (1960) defined corporate social responsibility as: "Businessmen's decisions and actions taken for reasons at least partially beyond the firm's direct economic or technical interest". Walton (1967) has also addressed many facets of CSR, and proposed a new concept of social responsibility recognizing the interaction between the corporation and society. He has further emphasized that these interactions need to be considered by all the stakeholders while pursuing their respective goals.

Further, Friedman (1962) conceptualized CSR as a social responsibility of business to use its resources and engage in activities designed to increase its profits so long as it stays within the rules of the game, which is particularly to engage in open and free competition without deception or fraud.

The term "corporate social responsibility" came into common use in the late 1960s and early 1970s after many multinational corporations formed the term stakeholder, meaning those on whom an organization's activities have an impact. It was used to describe corporate owners beyond shareholders (Freeman 1984).

2.3.3 Period of Rapid Growth in the Concept of CSR During 1970s

The decade of 1970s witnessed a significant growth in the concept of CSR by bringing new concepts such as corporate social responsiveness (Ackerman 1973; Ackerman and Bauer 1976), corporate social performance (CSP), and social responsibility.

In the beginning of 1970s, Friedman (1970) argued that the social responsibility of business is to increase its profits meeting the shareholder value maximisation approach which is referred to as capitalism. He further extends the capitalism argument to account for social responsibility as "there is one and only one social responsibility of business—to use it resources and engage in activities designed to increase its profits so long as it stays within the rules of the game, which is to say, engages in open and free competition without deception or fraud." The scholars from psychology and philosophy continued to provide refined concepts of CSR. For example, Johnson (1971) describes CSR as conventional wisdom where "a socially responsible firm is one whose managerial staffs balance a multiplicity of interests. Instead of striving only for larger profits for its stockholders, a responsible enterprise also takes into account employees, suppliers, dealers, local communities, and the nation." Later, Sethi (1975) distinguishes between CSP, CSR and corporate behaviours by conceptualising the 'dimensions of corporate social performance', 'social obligation', 'social responsibility', and 'social responsiveness' respectively. He further argues that the social responsibility implies synchronising the corporate behaviour with prevailing social norms, values, and expectations of performance.

Using a sample of major U.S. corporations who were engaged into some form of the activities that can be described in the area of social responsibility Eilbirt and Parket (1973), Parket and Eilbirt (1975) found that company size is positively related to the social responsibility efforts and the usual activities undertaken by most of the firms were related to contribution to education and arts. The corporations involved in activities which they consider socially responsible, were interested in making these activities widely known as well.

Hay and Gray (1974) conceptually divided the notion of social responsibility into three historical phases—"Phase I, the profit maximizer style; Phase II, the trusteeship style; and Phase III, the quality of life style. Phase III values will become more accepted by business managers of the future."

Carroll (1979) made a landmark contribution in the development of CSR concept as he proposed a four-part definition of corporate social responsibility which was embedded in a conceptual model of corporate social performance (CSP). The definition of CSR as proposed by Carroll can be stated as: "the social responsibility of business encompasses the economic, legal, ethical, and discretionary expectations that society has of organizations at a given point in time."

The four part framework of CSR as proposed by Carroll (1979) was widely accepted during this period and fully addresses the entire range of obligations business has to society: economic, legal, ethical, and discretionary. These four basic expectations categorize the social responsibilities of businesses in a more exhaustive manner. He further emphasises each responsibility is one part of the total social responsibility of business, giving a definition that completely reflects the societal expectation from the business.

The first and foremost social responsibility, the "economic responsibility", of business is to produce goods and services that society wants and to sell these at a profit. While pursuing the economic responsibilities, the society expects businesses to fulfil its legal responsibilities i.e. operating its activities within the framework of legal requirements. Although the economic and legal responsibilities involve certain ethical formal norms, there are additional behaviors and activities that are not necessarily imposed by law but nonetheless are expected of business by the members of society. These voluntary actions are guided only by a business' desire to engage in social roles and not necessarily governed by the law. Finally, "discretionary responsibilities" are the most convoluted ones and are left to individual judgment and choices.

However, Carroll (1991) revisited his 1979 framework to provide a more specific definition of discretionary component as philanthropic and suggesting that it embraced "corporate citizenship." He had succinctly put his argument as: "For CSR to be accepted by the conscientious business person, it should be framed in such a way that the entire range of business responsibilities is embraced. It is

Fig. 2.2 Pyramid model of CSR. *Source* Adapted from Carroll (1991)

suggested here that four kinds of social responsibilities constitute total CSR: economic, legal, ethical and philanthropic. Furthermore, these four categories or components of CSR might be depicted as a pyramid with economic responsibility being the foundation of the pyramid as shown in Fig. 2.2. To be sure, all of these kinds of responsibilities have always existed to some extent, but it has only been in recent years that ethical and philanthropic functions have taken a significant place."

Friedman (1970) attempted to find how a company is established and for what goal it operates and found that the main objective is profit. As profit is the most important thing, then the objective of business is merely to be responsible for the increasing of shareholders' wealth.

2.3.4 Stakeholder Theory and Business Ethics as CSR in 1980s

In the 1980s, the focus on developing new or refined definitions of CSR dominated the academic research on CSR. The concepts and themes such as corporate social responsiveness, corporate social performance, public policy, business ethics, and stakeholder theory and management were brought into recast the core concern of the CSR.

Summarizing the existing CSR debate, Jones (1980) argued that it is very difficult to reach consensus as to what constitutes socially responsible behaviour and therefore CSR ought to be seen as a process but not as a set of outcomes. Later, Muirhead (1999) categorized the period from the mid-1950s to mid-1980s as a period of 'growth and expansion' of corporate contributions. Further, Tuzzolino and Armandi (1981) proposed a microanalytic foundation for organizational analysis, using a paradigm taken from need theory. They presented a taxonomic construct to assess corporate performance proposing a yardstick to monitor its social responsibility. They further argued that the CSR can be easily motivated and operationalized in the context of an organizational-need hierarchy.

Two very important 'alternative themes' of CSR that developed during the 1980s' were stakeholder theory and business ethics mostly from the contributions of Freeman (1984) and Wartick and Cochran (1985).

As observed by Freeman (1984): "Our current theories are inconsistent with both the quantity and kinds of change that are occurring in the business environment of the 1980s…A new conceptual framework is needed." It was further developed by Freeman and Velamuri (2005) as a stakeholder approach to CSR to broaden the concept of business beyond its traditional economic roots, by defining stakeholders as—any group or individual who is affected by or can affect the achievement of an organization's objectives. Based on the stakeholder approach they proposed CSR as Company Stakeholder Responsibility which involves four levels of commitment to this new CSR, and have suggested ten principles that can help executives and business thinkers begin to apply this approach.[1]

Wartick and Cochran (1985) examined social issues management as a dimension of corporate social performance and concluded that the corporate social performance model is valuable for business and society study. Studies analysing the relationship between corporate social responsibility and firm profitability were also undertaken during this period. Epstein (1987) provided a definition of CSR relating social responsibility, responsiveness, and business ethics. He argued that these three concepts dealt with closely related, even overlapping, themes and concerns and defined CSR as the following: "Corporate social responsibility relates primarily to achieving outcomes from organizational decisions concerning specific issues or problems which (by some normative standard) have beneficial rather than adverse effects on pertinent corporate stakeholders. The normative correctness of the products of corporate action have been the main focus of corporate social responsibility."

1980s was mainly marked by the stakeholder theory which was further developed into a more holistic approach in 2000s to describe the concepts of CSR. March and Simon (1958), while developing the stakeholder theory further argued that the relationship between a company and its stakeholders is reciprocal as the stakeholders deliver contributions for the company to meet their interests and the company reward them benefits in return.

The main contributions are from Freeman (1984, 1994), Evan and Freeman (1988), Donaldson and Preston (1995), Freeman and Phillips (2002), Phillips et al. (2003) considers fiduciary duties towards stakeholders of the firm. Further its application requires reference to some moral theory (Kantian, Utilitarianism, theories of justice, etc.). For certain organizations frameworks like The Global Sullivan Principles and UN Global Compact universal rights are considered as

[1]For details see Freeman and Velamuri (2005) Annexure I and II.

CSR as they view CSR as to be framed as human rights, labour rights and respect for the environment that a company should possess. Achieving human development considering present and future generations as sustainable development are mainly highlighted as CSR by the World Commission on Environment and Development (Brutland Report; Gladwin et al. 1995). Finally, orientation towards the common good of society is described as CSR by Alford and Naughton (2002); Garriga and Mele (2004); and Kaku (1997).

Several authors then referred this stakeholder theory and created some new CSR models. These are Sustainable Development, Stewardship Theory, Triple Bottom Line, DNA of CSR2.0 Model, Practitioner-based model of societal responsibilities, value creation model of CSR and consumer drive corporate responsibility respectively.

In order to have a long-term perspective, Stakeholder Theory is further developed as Sustainable Development Theory which is defined by World Commission on Economic and Development as "development that meets the needs of the present without compromising the ability of future generations to meet their own needs". This definition emphasizes the concept in the balance between present and future dimensions. Hawken (1993) aligns this theory with his argument that business can harm the environment, but on the other hand, business is also crucial to solve sustainability problem of environment.

Nearly after two decades, Gechev (2005) observed that this concept consider both of short-term and long-term developments. Further Maples defines Sustainable Development as a combination between innovation and conservation. It is about doing innovation to respond the recent prompt changes while conserving socio-economical systems to get the balance of ecosystem. Sustainability is an important indicator of a company's performance in a long-term dimension (Maples 2005). The notion of important relationship between business and environment was then started to play in the Sustainable Development Theory. This theory then further developed into some new models, i.e. Triple Bottom Line, Sustainable Development Model and The DNA of CSR 2.0 Model.

2.3.5 CSR in Business Practice During 1990s

During the late 1980s and into the 1990s, corporate philanthropy expanded considerably starting from the pyramid model depicted by Carroll (1991) which further inspires some new novel models, such as Triple Bottom Line, Value Creation Model of CSR and The Model of Consumer Driven Corporate Responsibility. Muirhead (1999) characterized this period of corporate contributions as 'diversification and globalization'.

Around this time Davis, Schoorman and Donaldson (1997) integrated agency theory to define the concept stewardship which further influenced the evolution of the concepts of CSR in future. The stewardship theory view managers as "stewards" of corporate assets, satisfying shareholders, and stakeholders. In contrast to the agency theory that argue that maximisation of shareholders interest require separation of board chair and CEO, stewardship theory argues shareholder value maximisation is achieved by shared positions of board chair and CEO (Donaldson and Davis 1991). Stewardship Theory further led to some new CSR models in the 21st century such as Sustainable Development Model and The Model of Consumer Driven Corporate Responsibility.[2]

Elkington (1998) formulated a concept of "triple bottom line" (TBL) using stakeholder theory to measure and manage the impact of CSR that reflects economic, social and environmental performance. More global companies appeared in the world economy, and management positions dedicated to corporate giving began proliferating on the organization charts of major companies and corporate social performance emerged as more encompassing measure of performance.[3] Most of the research in 1990s evolved around the themes of: CSP, stakeholder theory, business ethics, sustainability and corporate citizenship.

The most significant advances to CSR in the 1990s came in the realm of business practice. The concept of CSR broadened from community involvement to an eventual and abiding concern for socially responsible products, processes, and employee relations. In 1992, a non-profit organisation called Business for Social Responsibility (BSR) was established to represent the initiatives and professionals having responsibility for CSR in their companies. BSR expanded the definition of CSR by encompassing various topics such as business ethics, community investment, environment, governance and accountability, human rights, marketplace and workplace. Further, BSR has also argued that terms such as corporate citizenship, business ethics, corporate accountability and sustainability can be used interchangeably to indicate CSR.

The 1990s was also characterized by the emergence of many different companies which have excellent reputations for their CSR practices. To name a few large companies like Nike, Merck, Coca-Cola, UPS, IBM, Prudential Insurance, Levi Strauss & Co., McDonald's, and Herman Miller, have developed significant CSR related reputations.

The 1990s also witnessed a similar trend in India wherein companies like Tata group, Nirma and Hindustan Unilever had created new business systems and products to meet the needs of under-served consumers, mostly from poor, rural areas.

---

[2]Other works based on integrated theories ranges from Sethi (1975), Ackerman (1973), Jones (1980), Vogel (2005) , Wartick and Mahon (1994). Preston and Post (1975, 1981) describe law and the existing public policy process as a reference for social performance. Wartick and Cochran (1985), Wood (1991) and Swanson (1995) propose role of social issues into assessment of corporate social performance. More recently the act of balancing the interests of the stakeholders of the firm as integrative theories as described by Mitchell et al. (1997), Agle et al. (1999), Rowley (1997).

[3]For example, Griffin and Mahon (1997) examined the relationship between corporate social performance and financial performance.

For example, Tata Steels introduced Lifeline express or Jeevan Rekha Express Train during 1990s which has reached out to more than 67,800 persons offering medical treatment. The company's entire range of healthcare services has been reaching out annually to 400,000 people in the interior villages of India through five hospitals and mobile health clinics.

2.3.6 Research on CSR in 21st Century

Twenty-first century has witnessed a shift in focus from theoretical construct towards the empirical research on the topics such as stakeholder theory, business ethics, sustainability, and corporate citizenship.

Husted (2000) presented a contingency theory of CSP in which he argued that CSP is a function of the nature of the social issue and its corresponding strategies and structures. This further leads to an integration of elements such as corporate social responsiveness, issues management, and stakeholder management. Further, Griffin (2000) argued that the existing research in related disciplines like marketing, human relations, psychology etc., can help to broaden our understanding of Corporate Social Performance. A different but relevant strand of literature described CSR as a signalling instrument to understand corporate commitment to social cases as a communication instrument within the framework of signalling models.

These frameworks essentially argue that CSR activities could possibly communicate relevant information over an enterprise to an uninformed actor, because they are afflicted with cost and hence can be deployed as a signal to reduce the asymmetric information premium (Jones and Murrel 2001; Fisman 2006).

Schwartz and Carroll (2003) refined the three-domain approach to CSR defined by Carroll (1979) by reducing the four categories of CSR into three as economic, legal, and ethical. Stormer (2003) suggested moving beyond the stakeholder model of the firm to an inter-systems model of business which requires modifying the view of corporations as autonomous or independent entities toward a view of firms as part of the communities that created them (Solomon 2004). This is further characterized as a shift from the 'egoic' view of the self as alienated towards the 'post-egoic' view of the organization self as interdependent (Driver 2006).

The twenty-first century also witnessed attention of global organisations to articulate best practices in CSR. For example, Organization for Economic Co-operation and Development (OECD) released the guidelines in corporate social responsibilities (OECD 2001). OECD released its first guidelines on CSR in 2001 for its member countries with voluntary initiatives. The report notes that there are significant divergences of commitment and management practices, even in narrow areas of application such as labor standards, environment, human rights, and fighting bribery. In addition to, research works such as Greenfield (2004), Maignan and Ralston (2002), McWilliams et al. (2006), Pearce and Doh (2005) provided theoretical and managerial discussions that argue "not only is doing good the right thing to do, but it also leads to doing better" (Bhattacharya and Sen 2004; Dunphy et al. 2003; Kotler and Lee 2005). Perrini (2005) analysed non-financial disclosure on CSR from corporate social, environmental and sustainability reports for ninety European companies and find that firms' disclosure is related to operational efficiency, maximum safety, environmental protection, quality & innovation, open dialogue, skill development, and responsible citizenship respectively.

Further, Habisch et al. (2005) documented the perspectives of CSR developments across Europe and argue that CSR is one of the most important topics for discussion for business people, politicians, trade unionists, consumers, NGOs, and researchers. In a specific study for UK, Moon (2004) presented how CSR evolved as a part of societal governance in the country which influenced the overall development of CSR in the European Union. Compared to the US, the notion of CSR in Europe is closely related to stakeholder responsibility. For example, Lyndenberg (2005) observes that the development of CSR in Europe was described as driven by "a long-term re-evaluation of the role of corporations in society".

Figure 2.3 describes the evolution of CSR in a chronological order from 1950s to 2000s. The figure also highlights the key researchers whose works have been highly cited regarding the progress of CSR from philanthropic interpretation to the business practices which accounts for the stakeholder approach.

The theories and concepts until the 21st century can be integrated as Sustainable Development theory which further augmented the existing concepts of CSR and TBL. For example, Aras and Crowther (2009) integrated the concept of Stewardship Theory into Triple Bottom Line to develop sustainable development model demonstrating the synergy and stewardship of financial, social and environmental resources to ensure sustainability. More specifically, the authors focus on internal and external interests of a company by asserting four aspects of CSR as follows:

- Economic aspect, to be the reason of the company's existence;
- Social aspect, to eradicate poverty and safeguard human rights;
- Environment, to preserve the nature for future generations;
- Organizational culture, to align the corporate and social values with individual values.

The integration of Stewardship Theory with TBL is further evolved into new models such as the DNA of CSR 2.0 Model, A Practitioner-Based Model of Societal Responsibilities and Consumer Driven Corporate Responsibilities Model.

The concept of DNA of CSR 2.0 is an integration of Stakeholder Theory and Sustainable Development by Visser et al. (2010a, b) conceiving this model as "spiralling, interconnected, non-hierarchical levels, representing economic, human, social and environmental systems, each with a twinned sustainability/responsibility manifestation: economic sustainability and financial responsibility; human sustainability and labour responsibility; social sustainability and community responsibility; and environmental sustainability and moral responsibility."

DNA of CSR 2.0 model combines the concepts of Connectedness "C", Scalability "S", and Responsiveness "R", along with Duality "2" and Circularity

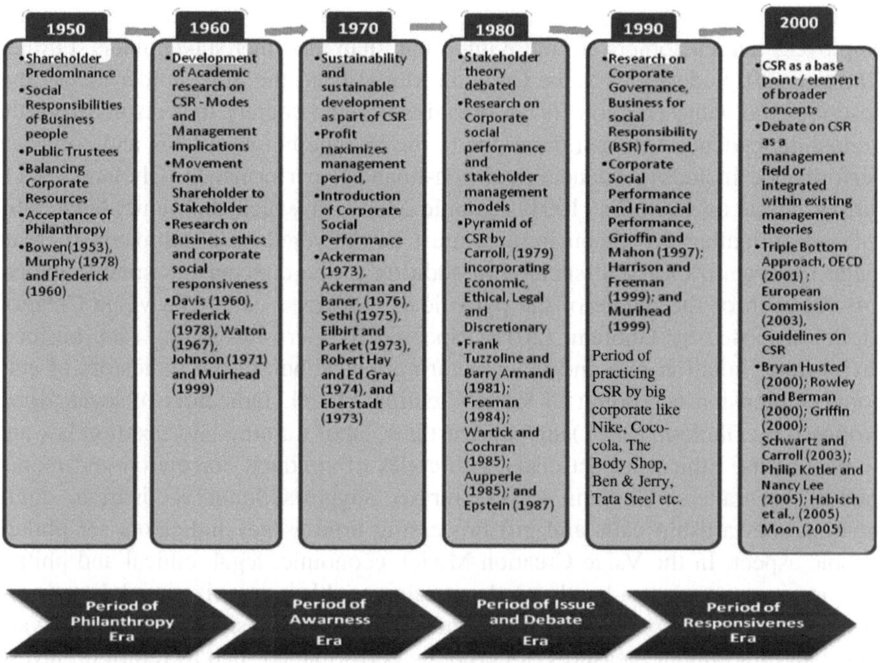

Fig. 2.3 Historical development of CSR in timeline. *Source* Authors' compilation from various literature surveys

for "0". Connectedness is about expressing multi-stakeholders relationships; Scalability indicates that CSR programs must be carried out by a company on a big scale and for a long-term duration; Responsiveness represents that a company must be responsive to deliver the needs of the community; Duality captures company's responsibility not only to economic aspect but to economic and social aspects as well. Finally, Circularity confirms the concept of sustainability.

A Practitioner-Based Model of Societal Responsibilities describes managers' perceptions where CSR is viewed in a relatively narrow sense. Pedersen (2010) describes that it is the focus on the TBL that brings out a more practitioner based model of social responsibilities. This further captures the differences in managers' view of CSR. For example, some of them view CSR in a reactive approach that CSR is carried out merely to comply with responsibility and avoid risk, while the others take the proactive approach to perceive CSR as an effort to make wider changes in society. Overall, managers view CSR as about producing good-quality products without doing harm to environment while creating value for the company and community. In such an approach the responsibilities of a company for products, people and environment are not only taken as its internal operations, but are also meant for creating value for the stakeholders rather than only for shareholders. While Practitioner-Based model builds on Stakeholder Theory, it does not take all stakeholders' interests as equally important and views CSR as a part of core business activities of a company where the managers perceive that employees and customers are more important than the other stakeholders. Further, Gholami (2011) develops Value Creation Model from the Stakeholder theory that describes the value creation for an organization and society that results from the mutual dependence between them due to the linkage between CSR and corporate performance including financial and non-financial performance. Gholami (2011) further builds on Carroll's (1991) Pyramid Model in which economic, legal, ethical and philanthropic responsibilities must be delivered by a company to create value for organization and society. In addition to the concept measurable indicators for each of the theme of the pyramid is explained under the Value Creation Model proposed by Gholami (2011). Specifically, personal saving rate, business saving rate, inflation rate and manufacturing lead time are the indicators of economic dimension according to Value Creation Model. Indicators of legal aspect proposed by Gholami (2011) are anti-trust law, labor training law, taxation law and human rights. Ethical aspect deals with codes of conduct, corruption and money laundering matters. Gholami (2011) further suggests donor acquisition, donor attrition, stewardship calls and gift processing time as key indicators for philanthropic aspect. In the Value Creation Model, economic, legal, ethical and philanthropic aspects are considered as independent variables; organizational dimensions of culture, technology, centralization and training are considered as control variables; and traditional measures of corporate performance such as return on investment (ROI), return on equity (ROE), Return on Asset (ROA), Operating Income (OI) and non-financial corporate performance including access of capital, business value, business savings, social value are considered as dependent variables respectively.

Finally, the Model of Consumer Driven Corporate Responsibility is coined by Claydon (2011). Similar to Value Creation Model, this model is also influenced by Carroll's Pyramid Model as economic approach is inevitably the main aspect of a company. The model further amalgamates concept of sustainability from the Sustainable Development Theory arguing that a company must remain profitable to be sustainable. Considering consumers as the most important stakeholders, this model argues that sustainable profitability can be achieved by ethical and responsible behaviour to its consumers. This model corroborates that CSR can be adopted to achieve competitive advantage by a company where customer base is not well established as well as to maintain profitable situation where the customer base is already established as the existing customers will continue demanding CSR from the company. Therefore, the company must respond to meet the CSR demand in order to remain reputable and profitable. This model shows a cycle that CSR adopted by a company will lead to the increased customer base which in turn means profitability. The profitability from CSR further leads to a greater reputation which can increase customer base. The increased customer base leads to the increased consumer demand for CSR, then it increases CSR adopted by the company.

2.4 Comprehensive Review of Surveys on Corporate Social Responsibility Around the World

In this section we capture the different aspects of CSR from the perspectives of various key stakeholders such as consumers, employees, and management decision makers like CEO's, along with the impact it creates on the society and environment in which the business operations are carried out. Further, in the emerging scenario, reporting of CSR activities are critical for all corporate across countries, we also bring out the status of CSR reporting and the way of communicating CSR to the public by corporate around the world.

This section is organised in a way to provide a clear picture of status of CSR from the perspective of consumers, employees, top management decision makers, and how companies started reporting their CSR. All these aspects are analysed across regions and various countries.

2.4.1 Consumers Perspective on CSR

In the corporate world, consumers are treated as most priority person and satisfying their needs and fulfilling their requirements would be the core objective any business entity. As corporate are loaded with an additional responsibility to take part in the social activities, this would trigger the expectation of consumers to yet another spectrum of understanding their priorities on CSR activities for the companies, their willingness towards CSR, and further their role in CSR emerge as an interesting areas to research both for the corporate and in academics.

A lot of surveys and studies have been conducted on assessing the consumer behaviour towards CSR. Researchers have established that the companies CSR programs indeed have a strong influence on consumers' attitudes and behaviour towards products and companies (Sen and Bhattacharya 2001). Customers use corporate reputation to assess products, with positive reputation resulting in higher perceptions of product or service quality (Jacoby et al. 1971; Shapiro 1983).

Consumers expectation on the corporate social responsibility role of companies have been surveyed in the Millennium Poll survey by Environics International in cooperation with the Prince of Wales Business Leaders Forum, during the year 1999, with a representative sample of 23,000 citizens across 23 countries. The major findings of the survey is that two out of three consumers want companies to contribute to broader societal goals that go beyond the historical role of making a profit, paying taxes, employing people and obeying the law. Over one in five consumers report that they have acted as ethical consumers, and almost as many again have considered doing so. It also highlighted that a higher amount of interest among the citizens in understanding the social and environmental impact of companies from all countries.

Social consciousnesses of the consumers about the product they buy are surveyed by Nielsen covering 28,000 online respondents from 56 countries around the world during 2012. The survey findings revealed that two thirds (66 %) of consumers around the world say they prefer to buy products and services from companies that have implemented programs to give back to society. That preference extends to other matters, too: they prefer to work for these companies (62 %), and invest in these companies (59 %). A smaller share, but still nearly half (46 %) say they are willing to pay extra for products and services from these companies, the "socially-conscious consumers," as defined and focused upon in the report. According to this survey, global, socially-conscious consumers tend to be younger: 63 % are under the age of 40, compared to 55 % of all respondents. In general, Nielsen's survey shows that younger consumers are more likely to spend extra for products and services from socially-responsible companies. Fifty-one percent of all respondents aged 15–39 are willing to pay extra for such products and services compared to 37 % of all respondents over age 40.

Further Nielsen conducted the second global survey on "Consumers Who Care And Say They'll Reward Companies with Their Wallets" during August 2013 around 58 countries. The survey results indicate that socially-conscious consumers care most about environmental sustainability. Around 66 % of socially conscious consumers identified environmental sustainability as a cause companies should support. More than 50 % of socially conscious consumers may be less obvious: improvements to science, technology and math education. Eradicating extreme poverty and hunger is also a priority for this segment, with 53 % of socially-conscious consumers believing brands should play a role in the cause.

Consumers willingness towards buying the products and services from a socially responsible company was surveyed by TNS Opinion and Social network among 27 Member States of the European Union and in Croatia, Israel, Turkey, Brazil, the United States, China and India during 2012 on citizen's view on how company influence society. Over 32,000 respondents have been covered under the survey. The findings of the survey showed that half of respondents said they would be willing to reward companies that give back to society by paying more for their goods and services. European respondents are much more likely to say that small and medium sized companies (71 %), rather than large companies (48 %), make efforts to behave in socially responsible ways. Respondents living in the EU and the US are the only ones who are more likely to think that small and medium companies are making efforts to behave responsibly towards society compared to large companies. In Brazil, India and Turkey the situation is reversed, with respondents more likely to say that large companies are making these efforts.

Europeans think that citizens themselves should take the lead role in influencing the actions of companies through their decisions about what they buy (49 %), followed by company management (40 %) and public authorities (36 %). Where as this decision was much higher among the respondents in India (70 %). Across the European Union, 40 % of Europeans think that companies pay more attention to their influence on society than they did 10 years ago. However, respondents in non-European countries like India resulted in 62 % a much higher compared with European and Non-European countries.

Similarly Cone Communications 2013 survey revealed that Just as consumers want companies to change, they also feel personally accountable for making responsible purchasing decisions. A mere 13 % feels they do not play any role in addressing social and environmental issues through their purchases, while one-in-five (21 %) consumers not only proactively seek out products and services they feel are responsible every time they shop, but also encourage others to do the same.

Priorities of the customers on the role of companies to do on CSR activities have been surveyed was carried out by IPSOS CSR Global Advisory among 24 countries with an international sample of 18,150 during 2013. On a global average it was found that customers mostly prioritize workplace safety, respect and adhere to local laws & rights and Contribute to the socioeconomic development of the countries where it operates. Whereas the least prioritized factor is fulfilling their financial and commercial targets to increase shareholder value, leave behind conditions for sustainable development after operations are closed and Maintain sustainable environmental practices. Indian Consumers also reflect the similar trend of priorities as of overall global average score.

Research suggests that companies may receive external benefits from implementing CSR policies. Field based and laboratory studies have found that CSR is linked to more favourable corporate evaluations, increased purchase behaviour (Lichtenstein et al. 2004), higher customer satisfaction and market value of a firm (Luo and Bhattacharya 2006) all of which is believed to translate into increased profitability for the corporation.

Cone Communications partnered with Echo Research to field out second comprehensive survey of global attitudes, perceptions and behaviours around CSR after 2011. They conducted an online survey of 10,287 consumers in 10 of the largest countries in the world. The survey broadly described "corporate social responsibility" to respondents in each country as "companies changing their business practices and giving their support to help address the social and environmental issues the world faces today." The survey findings reveal that globally 22 % opinioned that companies create impact on CSR whereas, 27 % believed that Consumers drive CSR, which shows that Consumers are more keen in bringing CSR. Similarly in India also showed the same trend with a higher percentage of 37 % believed that of company and 52 % believed that consumers drive CSR.

2.4.2 Employee Perceptions of Corporate Social Responsibility

There is also some evidence that CSR is beneficial because as with customer's willingness and acceptance of CSR activity also improves employees' perceptions of the company. When a company has CSR initiatives, employees are more proud of and committed to that organization. A study conducted by Brammer et al. (2007) also support this finding: employees' perceptions of their organizations' concern for community and environment is linked to their level of organizational commitment. Even after controlling for a whole host of relevant variable, perceptions of CSR make a unique and positive contribution to overall commitment. That is, the higher an employee rates their organization's corporate citizenship, the more committed they are to the organization.

Society for Human Resource Management conducted a pilot study on Corporate Social Responsibility Survey among Human Resource professionals employed by organizations operating in the United States, Australia, India, China, Canada, Mexico and Brazil during 2007. The survey findings revealed that Brazil reported the highest rate of organization participation in corporate social responsibility practices and where as in contrast China reported the lowest rate of participation in corporate social responsibility practices. Human Resource professionals from India who were employed by large or medium organizations reported that their organizations participated in donating/collecting money for natural disasters than those from small organizations.

2.4.3 CEO's Perspective on CSR

According to the survey of 766 United Nations Global Compact (UNGC) member CEOs, Accenture CEO Study Project Lead 2010, CEOs around the world are starting to see the shape of a new era of sustainability coming into view. In the face of rising global competition, technological change and the most serious economic downturn in nearly a century, corporate commitment to the principles of sustainability remains strong throughout the world. The major highlights of the survey are: Nearly one third of the respondents cited brand, trust and reputation as the top three factors followed by revenue growth and cost reduction as driving force for them to take action on sustainability issues. Among the development issues, education issues dominate climate change as crucial factor considered as the most important issue to address for the success of their business. And further all most all the respondents believe in integrating sustainability issues through their supply chain and also in the strategy and operation of their company.

PricewaterhouseCoopers (PwC) had made a global survey on CEOs in its 16th annual global survey during 2013 with 1330 CEOs interviews in 68 countries. The survey reported highest confidence in CSR reputation amongst North American CEOs, with 64 % feeling strongly that the public perceives their company as a positive social performer and 30 % feeling somewhat guarded confidence. Asia-Pacific CEOs have the lowest confidence in public perception of their companies as positive social performers, with only 28 % feeling strongly confident and 54 % feeling more cautiously confident.

The PwC survey results highlighted that about 75 % of CEOs in India are planning to strengthen their engagement with local communities, 72 % with the media and 59 % with NGOs. Forty-eight percent of CEOs in India (31 % globally) are also increasing their focus on volunteering and community work. Their attention to reducing the environmental footprint is almost on par with the global number; 44 % in India as opposed to 48 % globally. More than half of the CEOs interviewed in India are encouraging a framework to support a culture of ethical behaviour.

The Unites States based Conference Board carried out a global survey during 2002 on the attitudes of CEOs to developments in corporate citizenship. The highlights of survey results were: Company traditions and values to act ethically and be a force for economic development are by far the most important drivers for corporate social investment throughout the world. CEOs in the United States, Brazil and Europe say that their efforts to create future success through citizenship initiatives have only been 'somewhat' effective to date. In other regions, especially in the Asia-Pacific region, CEOs see their results as 'not very' effective.

2.5 Conclusion

The objective of this chapter is to highlight the evolution of the concepts of the corporate social responsibility around the world. Specifically, we focus on theoretical framework underpinning the corporate social responsibility. We also review various definitions highlighting some of the most widely used definitions which are exhaustive in nature. We conclude the chapter by providing a summary of various surveys conducted across the world by various agencies to understand the nature of CSR spending from differing perspectives of employees, consumers and management.

This chapter highlights the evolution of the concept of the corporate social responsibility around the world into phases of development of the concepts. There is no "one definition fits all" concept for CSR and therefore, specific definitions have evolved based on the institutional development, awareness about social issues and organizational behaviour. CSR is embedded in the management sciences with new constructs and linkages with organisational behaviour are evolving. The chapter also provides the comprehensive summary of some recent surveys on CSR activities to capture the perspectives of consumers, employees and management.

Against this backdrop the following chapter provides a detailed discussion on the relevant guidelines and best practices across the globe.

References

Ackerman RW (1973) How companies respond to social demands. Harvard Bus Rev 51(4):88–98

Ackerman RW, Bauer RA (1976) Corporate social responsiveness. Reston, Reston, VA

Agle BR, Mitchell RK, Sonnenfeld JA (1999) Who Matters To CEOs? An Investigation of Stakeholder Attributes and Salience, Corporate Performance and CEO Values. Acad Manage J 42(5):507–525

Alford H, Naughton M (2002) Beyond the shareholder model of the firm: working toward the common good of a business. In: Cortright SA, Naughton MJ (eds) Rethinking the purpose of business, University of Notre Dame Press, IN: Notre Dame, pp 27–47
Aras G, Crowther D (2009) The durable corporation: strategies for sustainable development (Gower Publishing Ltd)
Aupperle KE, Carroll AB, Hatfield JD (1985) An empirical investigation of the relationship between corporate social responsibility and profitability. Acad Manage J 28:446–463
Bhattacharya CB, Sen S (2004) Doing better at doing good: when, why, and how consumers respond to corporate social initiatives. Calif Manage Rev 47(1):9–24
Bowen HR (1953) Social responsibilities of the businessman. Harper & Brothers, New York
Brammer S, Millington A, Rayton B (2007) The Contribution of corporate social responsibility to organisational commitment. Int J Hum Resource Manage 18(10):1701–1719
Brown JA, Forster WR (2013) CSR and stakeholder theory: a tale of Adam Smith. J Bus Ethics 112(2):301–312
Carroll AB (1979) A three-dimensional conceptual model of corporate social performance. Acad Manage Rev 4:497–505
Carroll A (1991) The pyramid of corporate social responsibility: toward the moral management of organizational stakeholders. Bus Horiz 34:39–48
Carroll AB (1999a) Corporate social responsibility evolution of a definitional construct. Bus Soc 38(3):268–295
Carroll AB (1999b) Corporate social responsibility: evolution of a definitional construct. Bus Soc 38(3):268–295
Carroll A (2006) Corporate social responsibility: a historical perspective. In: Epstein MJ, Hanson KO (eds) The accountable corporation, vol 3. Praeger Publishers, Westport, pp 3–30. Buchholtz, 2006. Business and society: ethics and stakeholder management, 6th edn. South-Western College Publishing/International Thompson Publishing, Cincinnati
Clark JM (1939) Social control of business. McGraw-Hill, New York
Claydon J (2011) A new direction for CSR: the shortcomings of previous CSR models and the rationale for a new model. Soc Responsib J 7(3):405–420
Cochran PL, Wood RA (1984) Corporate social responsibility and financial performance. Acad Manage J 27(1):42–56
Davis K (1960) Can business afford to ignore social responsibilities? Calif Manage Rev II:70–76
Davis JH, Schoorman FD, Donaldson L (1997) Toward a stewardship theory of management. Acad Manage Rev 22(1): 20–47
Donaldson T, Preston LE (1995) The stakeholder theory of the corporation: concepts, evidence, and implications. Academy of management review 20(1):71
Driver M (2006) Beyond the stalemate of economics versus ethics: corporate social responsibility and the discourse of the organizational self. J Bus Ethics 66:337–356
Dunphy D, Griffiths A, Benn S (2003) Organizational change for corporate sustainability. Routledge, London
Eilbert H, Parket IR (1973) The current status of corporate social responsibility. Bus Horiz 16:5–14
Elkington J (1998) Cannibals with forks: the triple bottom line of 21st century business (New Society Publishers)
Epstein EM (1987) The corporate social policy process: beyond business ethics, corporate social responsibility, and corporate social responsiveness. Calif Manage Rev 29:99–114
Evan WM, Freeman RE (1988) A stakeholder theory of the modern corporation: kantian capitalism. In: Beauchamp TL, Bowie NE (eds) Ethical theory and business, 3rd edition (Englewood Cliffs). pp 97–106
Frederick WC (1960) The growing concern over business responsibility. Calif Manage Rev 2:54–61
Frederick WC (2006) Corporation be good: the story of corporate social responsibility. Dog Ear Publishing, Indianapolis
Freeman RE (1984) Strategic management: a stakeholder approach. Pitman, Boston

Freeman RE (1994) The politics of stakeholder theory: some future directions. Business ethics quarterly 4:409–421

Freeman RE, Phillips RA (2002) Stakeholder theory: a libertarian defense. Business ethics quarterly 12(3):331–350

Freeman RE, Velamuri SR (2005): A new approach to CSR: company stakeholder responsibility. In: Kakabadse A, Morsing M (eds) Corporate Responsibility, Palgrave Macmillan, UK

Friedman M (1962) Capitalism and freedom. University of Chicago Press, Chicago

Friedman M (1970) The social responsibility of business is to increase profits. N Y Times Mag 32–33, 122–126, Sept 2013

Garriga E, Mele D (2004) Corporate social responsibility theories: mapping and territory. J Bus Ethics 53:51–74

Gechev R (2005). Sustainable development. Economic aspect, University Press

Gholami S (2011) Value creation model through corporate social responsibility (CSR). Int J Bus Manag 6(9)

Gladwin TN, Kennelly JJ, Tara-Shelomith K (1995) Shifting paradigms for sustainable development: implications for management theory and research. Acad Manage Rev 20(4):874–907

Gond J-P, Moon J (2011) Corporate social responsibility in retrospect and prospect: exploring the life-cycle of an essentially contested concept, No. 59-2011 ICCSR research paper series—Routledge major work on corporate social responsibility

Greenfield WM (2004) In the name of corporate social responsibility. Bus Horizons 47(1):19–28

Griffin JJ (2000) Corporate social performance: research directions for the 21st century. Bus Soc 39(4):479–491

Griffin JJ, Mahon JF (1997) The corporate social performance and corporate financial performance debate: twenty-five years of incomparable research. Bus Soc 36:5–31

Habisch A, Jonker J, Wegner M, Schmidpeter R (eds) (2005) Corporate social responsibility across Europe. Springer, Berlin

Hawken P (1993) The ecology of commerce. Weidenfeld & Nicholson, London

Hay R, Gray E (1974) Social responsibilities of business managers. Acad Manage J 17:1

Husted BW (2000) A contingency theory of corporate social performance. Bus Soc 39(1):24–48

Jacoby J, Olson JC, Haddock RA (1971) Price, Brand Name, and Product Composition Characteristics as Determinants of Perceived Quality. J Appl Psychol 55:570–579

Johnson HL (1971) Business in contemporary society: framework and issues. Wadsworth Publishing Co., Inc., Belmont

Jones TM (1980) Corporate social responsibility revisited, redefined. Calif Manage Rev 59–67 (Spring)

Jones R, Murrell AJ (2001) Signaling positive corporate social performance: an event study of family-friendly firms. Bus Soc 40(1):59–78

Kaku R (1997) The path of kyosei'. Harvard Bus Rev 75(4):55–62

Kotler P, Lee N (2005) Corporate social responsibility: doing the most good for your company and your cause. Wiley, Hoboken

Lichtenstein DR, Drumwright ME, Braig BM (2004) The effect of corporate social responsibility on customer donations to corporate-supported nonprofits. J Marketing 68(10):16–33

Luo X, Bhattacharya CB (2006) Corporate social responsibility, customer satisfaction, and marketvalue, J Marketing 70(4): 1–18

Lydenberg SD (2005) Corporations and the public interest: guiding the invisible hand. Berrett-Koehler Publishers Inc., San Francisco

Maignan I, Ralston D (2002) Corporate social responsibility in Europe and the U.S.: insights from businesses' self-presentations. J Int Bus Stud 33(3):497–514

Maples AD (2005) Sustainable development. New Appl Sci J 27:1083–1086

March JG, Simon HA (1958) Organizations. New-York: John Wiley and sons

McWilliams A, Siegel DS, Wright PM (2006) Corporate social responsibility: strategic implications. J Manage Stud 43(1):1–18

Mitchell RK, Agle BR, Wood DJ (1997) Toward a theory of stakeholder identification and salience: defining the principle of who and what really counts. Acad Manage Rev 22(4):853–886

Mohan A (2003) Strategies for the management of complex practices in complex organizations: a study of the transnational management of corporate responsibility. Unpublished doctoral dissertation, University of Warwick, United Kingdom

Moon, J. (2004). CSR in the UK: an explicit model of business – society relations. In: Habisch A, Jonker J, Wegner M, Schmidpeter R (eds) CSR across Europe. Springer, Berlin, pp 51–65

Muirhead SA (1999) Corporate contributions: the view from 50 years. The Conference Board, New York

Murphy PE (1978) An evolution: corporate social responsiveness. Univ Mich Bus Rev

Organization for Economic Co-operation and Development (OECD) (2001) Corporate responsibility: private initiatives and public goals. OECD, Paris

Parket IR, Eilbirt H (1975) Social responsibility: the underlying factors. Bus Horiz XVIII:5–10

Pearce JA, Doh JP (2005) High-impact collaborative social initiatives. MIT Sloan Manage Rev 46(3):30–39

Pedersen ER (2010) Modelling CSR: how managers understand the responsibilities of business towards society. J Bus Ethics 91(2):155–166

Perrini F (2005) Book review of corporate social responsibility: doing the most good for your company and your cause. Acad Manage Perspect 90–93 (May)

Phillips RA, Freeman RE, Wicks AC (2003) What stakeholder theory is not. Bus ethics quart 13(4):479–502

Preston LE, Post JE (1975) Private management and public policy: the principle of public responsibility. Prentice-Hall, Englewood Cliffs

Preston LE, Post JE (1981) Private management and public policy. In: california management review. 23(3):56–63

Rowley TJ (1997) Moving beyond dyadic ties: A network theory of stakeholder influences. Acad Manage Rev 22:887–910

Schwartz MS, Carroll AB (2003) Corporate social responsibility: a three domain approach. Bus Ethics Q 13(4):503–530

Sen S, Bhattacharya CB (2001) Does doing good always lead to doing better? consumer reactions to corporate social responsibility. J Mark Res 38(5):43–62

Sethi SP (1975) Dimensions of corporate social performance: an analytic framework. Calif Manage Rev 17:58–64 (Spring)

Shapiro C (1983) Premium for high quality products as returns to reputations. Quart J Econ 98(4):659–679

Stormer F (2003) Making the shift: moving from “ethics pays” to an inter-systems model of business. J Bus Ethics 44(4):279–288

Swanson DL (1995) Addressing a theoretical problem by reorienting the corporate social performance model. Acad Manage Rev 20:43–64

Tuzzolino F, Armandi BR (1981) A Need-hierarchy framework for assessing corporate social responsibility. Acad Manage Rev 6:21–28

Visser W (2010a) CSR 2.0: From the age of greed to the age of responsibility. In: Sun W et al (eds) Reframing corporate social responsibility, Lessons from the global financial crisis, Emerald, Bingley

Visser W (2010b) The age of responsibility: CSR 2.0 and the new DNA of business. J Bus Systems, Govern Ethics 5(2):7–22

Vogel DJ (2005) Is there a market for virtue? the business case for corporate social responsibility. Cal manage rev 47(4):19–45

Waddock SA, Graves SB (1997) The corporate social performance–financial performance link. Strat Mgmt J 18: 303–319

Walton CC (1967) Corporate social responsibilities. Belmont, CA: Wadsworth

Wartick SL, Cochran PL (1985) The evolution of the corporate social performance model. Acad Manage Rev 10:758–769

Wartick SL, Mahon JF (1994) Toward a substantive definition of the corporate issue construct a review and synthesis of the literature. Bus Soc 33(3):293–311

Wood DJ (1991) Corporate social performance revisited. Acad Manage Rev 16:691–718

Chapter 3
Corporate Social Responsibility—Guidelines and Best Practices

3.1 Introduction

We provide a comprehensive review of various principles and guidelines of CSR around the world describing the multi-dimensionality and the interdisciplinary approach to undertake our study in chapters that follow. The chapter summarizes all the relevant guidelines and best practices across the globe based on various published surveys and reports. We first discuss the best practices across advanced and emerging economies. Secondly, we provide a summary of guidelines that governs the CSR practices as proposed by various organisations such as UN, OECD etc.

As succinctly documented by Kolah (2015), there are wide-spread differences in understanding CSR and key focus areas of CSR activities across the spectrum of countries ranging from developed; developing and emerging economies. For example, CSR had been a well defined concept in many countries such as USA, UK and Canada where firms had developed the CSR strategies in response to a growing rise of issues such as sustainable investments as well as a marketing instrument to develop brand awareness. Further, most of the listed companies in Japan report CSR strategies and initiatives in their annual CSR report. On the other hand, firms in Israel fail to see the need to develop and provide specific information on CSR activities.

CSR in Asian economies such as Hong Kong and Singapore represents transparency and accountability, taking account of workplace and community issues, as well as ensuring strong development and opportunities for their workforce. There is also a significant variation across countries in motivation of CSR activities. For example while most of the countries view CSR as an integral part of their business strategies; countries such as India being dominated by family owned firms often attribute CSR to charity and philanthropic activities.

S.N. Bhaduri and E. Selarka, *Corporate Governance and Corporate Social Responsibility of Indian Companies*, CSR, Sustainability, Ethics & Governance, DOI 10.1007/978-981-10-0925-9_3

3.2 Global Principles and Guidelines on Corporate Social Responsibility

Global organisations such as UN, OECD have developed guidelines, frameworks, principles and tools based on the larger concepts of sustainability or business responsibility as a notion of CSR.

3.2.1 Business and the Millennium Development Goals (BDGs)

BDGs provide a conceptual framework for business, civil society and government to focus their efforts on the most urgent development issues by describing the following goals:

1. Eradicate extreme poverty and hunger
2. Achieve universal primary education
3. Promote gender equality and empowerment of women
4. Reduce child mortality
5. Improve maternal health
6. Combat HIV/AIDS, malaria, and other diseases
7. Ensure environmental stability
8. Develop a global partnership for development.

3.2.2 United Nations Global Compact (UNGC)

The Global Compact—a voluntary UN initiative provides a set of objectives that defines a framework for businesses to align their operations and strategies in the areas of human rights, labour, the environment and anti-corruption. The objectives are:

- Mainstream the ten universally accepted principles in the aforementioned areas
- Catalyse actions in support of broader UN goals, such as the Millennium Development Goals (MDGs).

UNGC is the largest corporate citizenship initiative to facilitate the adoption of sustainable and socially responsible policies by businesses around the world. The ten principles of the UN Global Compact have been derived from various UN conventions such as the Universal Declaration of Human Rights, ILO's Declaration on Fundamental Principles and Rights at Work, the Rio Declaration on environment and development, and the UN Convention against Corruption. Following ten principles specifically cover four broad areas: Human Rights, Labour, Environment and Anti-Corruption:

1. Businesses should support and respect the protection of internationally proclaimed human rights;
2. To make sure that they are not complicit in human rights abuses.
3. Businesses should uphold the freedom of association and the effective recognition of the right to collective bargaining;
4. The elimination of all forms of forced and compulsory labour;
5. The effective abolition of child labour; and
6. The elimination of discrimination in respect of employment and occupation.
7. Businesses should support a precautionary approach to environmental challenges;
8. To undertake initiatives to promote greater environmental responsibility; and
9. To encourage the development and diffusion of environmental friendly technologies.
10. Businesses should work against corruption in all its forms, including extortion and bribery.

Further, Global Compact Self Assessment Tool provides a guide designed for all companies irrespective of their size and sector in which it is operating. The tool is specially designed to guide companies which are committed to maintain the social and environmental standards within their respective operations. The tool consists of 45 questions with a set of three to nine indicators for each question across the broad themes covered under UNGC: human rights, labour, environment and anti-corruption. In addition to these four sections, the tool includes the "management" section.

The questions on human rights are based on the UN guiding principles for the states and businesses to fulfil their existing obligations towards respecting and protecting human rights. These principles are specified as global standards for addressing the risk of human rights violation related to business activity. In addition, guidelines are recommended for the circumstances when these laws are breached or the guidance is not adhered to.

For small companies, this tool acts as a measure of the company's performance in all areas of the UN Global Compact and how well these issues are managed within a company. On the other hand, for large organisations, this tool helps to continuously improve existing policies and systems, engage subsidiaries, suppliers or other stakeholders, and improves internal and external reporting.

3.2.3 New Guiding Principles on Business and Human Rights

The United Nations Human Rights Council endorsed a new set of Guiding Principles for Business and Human Rights to provide a global standard for preventing and addressing the risk of adverse impacts on human rights in business activities by recommending how States and businesses should implement the UN principles in "Protect, Respect and Remedy" Framework in order to better manage business and human rights challenges. The 'State Duty to Protect' framework provides guidelines for governments to provide clear expectations and consistencies in rules for business in relation to human rights. The 'Corporate Responsibility to Respect' framework outlines a set of guidelines for companies to understand and demonstrate respect for human rights in their businesses. The 'Access to Remedy' principles ensure adequate accountability and effective redress, judicial and non-judicial in case of any harm to people caused by business activities.

3.2.4 OECD Guidelines: Multinational Enterprises

OECD (2008) Guidelines for multinational enterprises elaborate on the principles and standards for responsible business conduct for multinational corporations covering areas such as employment, human rights, environment, information disclosure, combating bribery, consumer interests, science and technology, competition and taxation. These guidelines provide standards for socially and environmentally responsible corporate behaviour, and also provide procedures for resolving disputes between corporations and communities or individuals adversely impacted by business activities.

This framework aims to help companies gain insight into their current CSR activities, assess its value and determine other CSR activities that can be further employed thereby providing a complete guideline, including an action plan with tasks, responsibilities and a communication strategy plan.

3.2.5 Europe Union Commission on CSR

The European Commission defines CSR as "the responsibility of enterprises for their impacts on society" (COM 2011) and highlights the principles that encourages that enterprise "should have in place a process to integrate social, environmental, ethical human rights and consumer concerns into their business operations and core strategy in close collaboration with their stakeholders". It further emphasises the following principles for CSR for its member countries:

- Human rights,
- Labour and employment practices[1]
- Environmental issues (such as biodiversity, climate change, resource efficiency, life-cycle assessment and pollution prevention), and
- Combating bribery and corruption.

[1]International Labour Organization Tripartite Declaration of Principles concerning Multinational Enterprises on Social Policy.

- Community involvement and development,
- The integration of disabled persons, and
- Consumer interests, including privacy, are also part of the CSR agenda and
- The promotion of social and environmental responsibility through the supply-chain, and the disclosure of non-financial information, are recognised as important cross-cutting issues.

3.3 Accounting Standards on Corporate Social Responsibility

This section highlights the accounting standards that enable organizations to become accountable, responsible and sustainable.

AccountAbility, a leading global organisation providing innovative solutions in corporate responsibility and sustainable development, which provides a framework for an organisation to address its sustainability challenges. The three essential components of this framework are AA1000 accountability principles standard (AA1000 APS), AA1000 assurance standard (AA1000AS) and The AA1000 Stakeholder Engagement (AA1000SE).

AA1000 APS provides an organisation with an internationally accepted freely available set of principles to frame and structure the way in which they understand, govern administer, implement, evaluate and communicate their accountability. AA1000 assurance standard (AA1000AS) provides a methodology for practitioners to evaluate the nature and extent to which an organisation adheres to the Accountability Principles AA1000APS. Finally, AA1000SE provides a framework to help organisations ensure stakeholder engagement processes are purpose driven, robust and deliver results.[2]

Further, Social Accountability International (SAI: SA8000), overseen by Social Accountability Accreditation Services (SAAS) is one of the world's first auditable social certification standard, based on ILO, UN and national law conventions. This certification standard propagates management system approach to ensure the protection of basic human rights of workers and apply socially acceptable practices in the workplace. SAI provides the accreditation based on the nine basic elements of this standard include (i) child labour (ii) forced and compulsory labour (iii) health and safety (iv) freedom of association and the right to collective bargaining (v) discrimination (vi) disciplinary practices (vii) working hours (viii) remuneration (ix) management systems. According to SAAS, there are 695 facilities in India

[2]For example, Vodafone Group Plc has adopted the AA1000AP standard by focussing on three broad areas such as inclusivity (stakeholder engagement to develop and implement a strategic approach to sustainability); materiality (assess the management effort required for each material issue and determine the content of sustainability reports) and responsiveness (respond with solutions to material issues and challenges).

that have been accredited with SA8000. Out of these, Aditya Birla Chemicals (India) Limited, Bhilai Steel Plant Steel Authority of India Limited, Birla tyres, Dr Reddy's Laboratories Limited and Reliance Infrastructure Limited figure prominently in the list of certified facilities within India.

More recently, ISO 26000 (2010) provides guidance to enable organisations to follow a holistic concept of social responsibility and sustainable development across six core areas of Human rights; Labour practices; Environment; Fair operating practices; Consumer issues; and Community involvement and development.

3.3.1 Social Return on Investments (SROI) Network

A framework on social generally accepted accounting principles (SGAAP) designed by SROI Network is also used to manage and understand the social, economic and environmental outcomes created by an organisation. SROI helps in understanding, managing and communicating the social value consistent with the objectives of all stakeholders' to enhance the social value or impact of a task as well as in managing risks, identifying opportunities and raising finances.

3.3.2 London Benchmarking Group Model (LBG) Model

Similarly many companies across the world adopt LBG's measurement model to assess the real value and impact of community investment to the business and society. LBG model provides the framework to the firm to understand the total amount of cash, time and in-kind invested within the community. It also enables companies to understand the geographic spread of community support and themes supported such as education, health and arts and culture. The framework further helps the companies to track their community programme supports consistent with their business goals such as building employee morale or creating reputational advantages. One salient point under LBG model is that it allows member companies to share data and best practices which in turn help in the benchmarking process.

3.3.3 The Principles for Responsible Investment (PRI)

PRI provides a set of voluntary principles for the firms to incorporate the environmental, social and corporate governance (ESG) issues into their investment decision-making. These issues are widely accepted to affect the performance of investment portfolios and therefore, institutional investors have developed these principles since 2005.

3.3.4 Transparency International (TI)

TI is the global civil society organisation is one of the leading institutions to fight against corruption by bringing people together across the globe which has perilous impact on men, women and children around the world. By bringing together relevant players from government, civil society, business and the media TI promotes transparency in elections, public administration, procurement and business conduct.

3.3.5 The Global Reporting Initiative (GRI)

GRI is a non-profit organization that promotes economic, environmental and social sustainability by designing a comprehensive sustainability reporting framework which is widely used around the world. India has been a focal point of GRI which believes that it will have a big sustainability impact. Therefore, GRI entered into a strategic alliance with Deutsche Gesellschaftfür Technische Zusammenarbeit (GTZ) in setting up the GRI Focal Point India into their IICA-GTZ CSR Initiative which provides guidance and support to local organizations to achieve standardized practice in sustainability reporting.

3.4 Reporting and Impact of CSR

Reporting of CSR by the corporate has become important since emergence of various mandatory and voluntary regulations & guidelines framed by various countries around the world. Chambers et al (2003) investigates the penetration of CSR reporting of top 50 companies in seven Asian countries namely India, Indonesia, Malaysia, the Philippines, Singapore, South Korea and Thailand to analyze the extent of CSR reporting within companies. Specifically, the article evaluates the extent of homogeneity and national distinctiveness in CSR across these countries with respect to their CSR priorities and modalities to achieve the same. Using various proxies to capture the differing levels of country specific CSR penetration, they investigate the impact of globalisation. In general, the paper reports that levels of CSR in Asia lag behind than that of the western countries. However, the paper also highlights the fact that many Asian countries have developed their own systems of CSR which is further driven through globalisation.

In another study, CSR Network surveyed 45 global and large companies of the European Union during 2000. The report reveals that over 90 % of these companies report their mission, vision and values, workplace climate, community involvement, local economic development, marketplace and environmental impact. The report further reveals that over half of the world's hundred largest firms produced Global Environmental Reports.

Recently KPMG International Survey on Corporate Responsibility (CR) Reporting was conducted during 2011 and 2013. The survey reports that the global average reporting rate has increased from 64 % in 2011 to 71 % in 2013 and there has been a dramatic increase in corporate reporting rates in Asia-Pacific over the last two years. The survey further reports that 71 % of companies based in Asia-Pacific now publish CR reports which is an increase of 22 % since 2011. It also highlights that due to a significant increase in CR reporting in Latin America, 76 % of companies in the Americas now report on CR compared to 73 % in Europe and 71 % in Asia-Pacific making Americas as the leading corporate reporting region. Further, the highest growth in CR reporting since 2011 has been witnessed by countries such as India (53 %), Chile (46 %), Singapore (37 %), Australia (25 %), Taiwan (19 %) and China (16 %) in 2013.

Further to understand the Impact of CSR on the Society and Environment, a study by Cone Communications along with Echo Research to conduct a comprehensive survey of global attitudes, perceptions and behaviours around CSR during 2013. The study is based on an online survey of 10,287 consumers in 10 largest countries in the world. The study reports that the majority of consumers feel both individuals and corporations have positive influence on social and environmental issues. The study further reports that around 22 % of consumers believe companies have made significant positive impact on social and environmental issues and around 27 % believes that consumers can have significant positive impact through their purchases.

Social identity theory (Tajfel and Turner 1979) has also been tested in the context of CSR. The theory defines a *group* based on people's self-conception as members of group which is formalized as social identity to explain intergroup behaviour. Drawing on social identity theory Brammer et al. 2007 investigate the relationship between organisational commitment and employee perceptions of CSR. Multidimensional construct of CSR is computed based on three aspects of employee perceptions: employee perceptions of community CSR, procedural justice in the organisation and the provision of employee training respectively. Using a sample of 4712 employees of a financial services company the article finds a positive relationship between three measures and affective organisational commitment after controlling for job satisfaction, leadership, age, tenure and gender.

Further, Reverte (2009) analysed the determinants of CSR disclosure practices by Spanish listed firms by investigating media exposure along with firm and industry characteristics. The paper finds that firms with larger size, operating in more environmentally sensitive industries and higher media exposure have significantly higher CSR ratings. In contrast, neither profitability nor leverage explains differences in CSR disclosure practices in Spanish listed firms. The most influential variable for explaining firms' variation in CSR ratings is media exposure, followed by firm size and industry. The study finds support for the legitimacy theory that argue that variables related to public or social visibility are relevant for explaining CSR disclosure practices of Spanish listed firms.

There exists a conceptual and practical gap existing between the developed and developing countries in relation to CSR which is termed as North-South 'CSR

Divide'. Gugler and Shi (2009) explores competitiveness and CSR engagement to suggesting that developing countries are changing their approaches to engage into proactive CSR to synchronize with their competitive position in global trade. The authors further suggest two policy proposals to bridge the CSR gap by improving CSR standard-setting participation from both sides of globe, and by recommending international investment legal framework to define corporate obligations in relating to CSR in a more explicit way. Using content analysis, Gamerschlag et al. (2010) construct a CSR disclosure index based on the Global Reporting Initiative (GRI) guidelines for 130 German listed companies to analyse the determinants of voluntary CSR disclosure. The authors find that consistent with the political cost theory, German companies' disclosures of CSR issues are affected by their size, industry, visibility, shareholder structure, and relationship with their US stakeholders. In addition, higher profitability is associated with more environmental disclosures. More recently Ghosh and Chakraborty (2014) argue that mandating CSR may not result into responsible business and suggest a framework where the concept of CSR should be understood in a sustainable development (SD) framework which integrates economic, ecological and social.

3.5 Conclusion

The chapter provides a comprehensive review of various principles and guidelines of CSR around the world describing the multi-dimensionality and the interdisciplinary approach that defined the concept of CSR. We summarize all the relevant guidelines and best practices across the globe based on various published surveys and reports. Further the chapter also discuss the best practices across advanced and emerging economies and provide a summary of guidelines that governs the CSR practices as proposed by various organisations such as UN, OECD etc.

In line with rest of the world, India has also witnessed evolution of CSR guidelines, codes and standards. The next chapter elaborates the historical evolution of Corporate Social Responsibility in a phased manner along with the insight on pre and post industrialisation and globalisation scenario in India.

References

Brammer S, Millington A, Rayton B (2007) The contribution of corporation social responsibility to organizational commitment. Int J Hum Res Manag 18(10):1701–1719

Chambers E, Chapple W, Moon J, Sullivan M (2003) CSR in Asia: A seven country study of CSR website reporting. ICCSR Research Papers No. 10

Gamerschlag R, Moller K, Verbeeten F (2010). Determinants of voluntary CSR disclosure: Empirical evidence from Germany. Rev of Manage Sci, 4

Ghosh A, Chakraborty C (2014) Beyond corporate social responsibility: Ethics in Action. Global Virtue Ethics Rev, 6(4):60–99

Gugler P, Shi JY (2009) Corporate social responsibility for developing country multinational corporations: lost war in pertaining global competitiveness? J Bus Ethics 87:3–24
Kolah (2015) Improving the performance of sponsorship. Routledge
Reverte C (2009) Determinants of corporate social responsibility disclosure ratings by spanish listed firms. J Bus Ethics 88:351–366
Tajfel H, Turner JC (1979) An integrative theory of intergroup conflict. In W. G. Austin & S. Worchel (eds) The social psychology of intergroup relations. Monterey: Brooks-Cole, pp 33–47

Chapter 4
Corporate Social Responsibility in India: Evolution and Progress of CSR and Regulations

4.1 Introduction

In previous chapter, we present the evolution of concepts of CSR across the globe and the selected regulations that recommend and govern the CSR practices. This chapter elaborates the historical evolution of Corporate Social Responsibility in a phased manner along with the insight on pre and post industrialisation and globalisation scenario in India. Further the chapter presents the guidelines to conduct CSR related activities.

The concept of social responsibility in business is not new in India. The country has a long tradition of corporate philanthropy and industrial welfare that has been put in practice since as long as 1800s. Business is known for not only creating excess wealth for its own, but also creates social and environmental concerns that are deep roots in the history of business in India (Gautam and Singh 2010). Particularly in number of family-based organisations, traditionally it has been set with a strong community ethos (Chendroyaperumal and Juliet 2009).

In India, Companies Act governs the activities of corporate entity which is amended since 1956. Recently, the Companies Act, 2013 introduced CSR provisions in the Act through amended Clause 135 and Schedule VII outlining various CSR activities that can be carried out by the Indian companies. This makes India unique and the first country in the world to mandate the CSR spending along with a framework to identify the potential CSR activities.

The chapter also provides a survey of empirical literature to understand the state of social responsibility of Indian firms. The chapter is organised as follows. Next section describes the historical evolution of CSR in India; Sect. 4.3 summarizes the principles and guidelines of CSR in India, Sect. 4.4 reviews case studies and empirical research on CSR.

S.N. Bhaduri and E. Selarka, *Corporate Governance and Corporate Social Responsibility of Indian Companies*, CSR, Sustainability, Ethics & Governance,
DOI 10.1007/978-981-10-0925-9_4

4.2 Evolution of Corporate Social Responsibility in India

India has a long tradition of corporate philanthropy and industrial welfare that has been put to practice since ancient times dating back to philosophers like Kautilya who had emphasized on moral practices and values while doing business in India (Kumar and Rao 1996). CSR has been informally practiced in ancient times in the form of charity to the poor and underprivileged section of society.

There are ample examples in Indian scriptures which highlights the importance of sharing one's earning with the underprivileged section of society. The tradition continues in the modern times with firms like Tatas, Birlas, Godrej, Bajajs, Singhanias and Modis practiced CSR by setting up charitable foundations, educational and healthcare institutions consistent with the strong community ethos. The corporate philanthropy involved funding projects for building schools, pilgrim rest houses, places of worship like temples, distributing relief items during disasters, helping the poor and empowering employees. In fact the Tata Group is credited for introducing 'social responsibility' among corporate houses in the country (Gupta 2007; Gautam and Singh 2010).

Although there has been a little documentation of social responsibility initiatives in India, particularly during the initial years, there has been a growing degree of companies that pay genuine attention to the principles of socially responsible behaviour, which are favoured by the customers and also preferred for their goods and services reflected in various studies (Millennium Poll Survey (conducted by Environics International in 2001); Sen et al. 1999; Flash Eurobarometer 2013; Nielsen 2012; IPSOS-Mori 2013).

This section presents the five distinct phases of CSR development in the Indian economy as Ethical (1800–1914); Trusteeship (1914–1960); Statist (1960–1980); Liberal (1980–1990) and Stakeholder (After 1990s).[1] Summary of these five phases of evolution of CSR in India is described in Table 4.1.

4.2.1 Ethical Approach (1800–1914): CSR as Charity and Philanthropy

Although there is no formal concept of CSR in this period, India not only witnessed a rich hub of merchandise trading in the world, but also the social engagement of wealthy merchants. The oldest form of CSR in India was predominately in the form of donations, charity and philanthropy. Hence, the first phase was mainly based on self-regulation of doing business characterized by culture, religion,

[1]Some authors classify this evolution into four phases wherein the period of privatization, liberalization and globalization is missing (Sundar 2000; Chahoud et al. 2007; Gupta 2012).

Table 4.1 Five phases of CSR development in India

Phase/period	Year	Nature of CSR strategies	Models/approach's
I/pre-industrialization	1800–1914	The oldest form of CSR was motivated by charity and philanthropy with direct influence from culture, religion, family tradition, and industrialization process	Ethical
II/industrialization	1914–1960	Dominated by the country's struggle for independence and influenced fundamentally by Gandhi's theory of trusteeship for consolidation and amplification of social development. Gandhi's reform programs which included activities that sought in particular the abolition of untouchability, women's empowerment and rural development	Ethical/trusteeship
III/post-industrialization	1960–1980	The paradigm of mixed economy with the emergence of legislation on labour and Environmental standards, affected the third phase of Indian CSR This phase is also characterized by a shift from corporate self regulation to strict legal and public regulation of business activities	Statist
IV/pre liberalisation	1980–1990	Indian companies and stakeholders began abandoning traditional philanthropic engagement and, to some extent, integrated CSR into a coherent and sustainable business strategy, partly adopting the multi stakeholder approach	Liberal
V/post liberalisation	1990–recent	Transformation from charity oriented approach to stakeholder oriented one. The target group is seen as a stakeholder in the community and is being forming an integral part of the company's success	Stakeholder

family values and tradition but also influenced by caste groups and political objectives. The tradition of wealth sharing of the big businessperson for social causes like setting up of temples, helping the society in getting over phases of famine, and epidemics by providing food and money to the poor and thus securing an integral position in the society was followed as a tradition. The approach towards CSR changed since 1850s when the large industrial families were inclined towards economic as well as social considerations.[2]

4.2.2 Trusteeship Approach (1914–1960)

During India's struggle for independence in 1914 Gandhi introduced the notion of "trusteeship", wherein the industrial houses establish trusts for the welfare of the common man. Trusts for schools, colleges and scientific institutions were established to undertake activities in line with Gandhi's attempt to abolish untouchability, encourage empowerment of women and rural development. The concept of "trusteeship" views businesses as stewards of society's resources and assets that the right of a capitalist is to accumulate and maintain her wealth for the welfare of the society (Gopinath 2005; Narayan 1966).

Theory of trusteeship resonates strongly with those founded in England and the United States in the late nineteenth and early twentieth centuries that later evolved into the concept of CSR (Masani 1956; Narayan 1996; Renold 1994). Further, Kumar et al. (2004) presents Gandhi's theory of trusteeship as an "ethical model" of CSR where companies commit voluntarily for public welfare.[3] Similar to philanthropy in the early industrialization phase, this phase was also characterized by the support for physical and social institutional infrastructure (Sood and Arora 2006). However in this period, such ideas were led by a nationalistic fervour and a vision of a free, progressive and modern India and not necessarily as social responsibility (Sundar 2000).[4]

---

[2]For example, Tata Groups is a leading provider of maternal and child health services, family planning, and has provided 98 % immunization in Jamshedpur. Tata Group also has an organized relief program in case of natural disasters, including long-term treatment and rebuilding efforts. It also supports education covering over 500 schools, and also is a benefactor of the arts and culture.

[3]Pachauri (2004) has established another connection between CSR and trusteeship emphasising on stewardship notion of ownership of capital wherein society provides opportunities to capitalists to manage resources which can be understood as trusteeship on behalf of society in general.

[4]The Tata group incorporated the principle of trusteeship not only through charity but also by establishing institutions like Tata Institute of Fundamental Research (TIFR) and Birla Institute of Technology and Science (BITS) towards creation of human resources and technological capability in this country. In addition, scholarships were provided to students to study overseas (J N Tata scholarship) and donations were made to global institutions to establish centres (Ratan Tata Foundation).

4.2.3 Statist Approach (1960–1980)

In 1960s there was a paradigm shift in the economy when India adopted the socialist and mixed economy framework with emergence of Public Sector undertakings (PSUs), state-owned companies. This framework was propagated by then prime minister Jawahar Lal Nehru and is recognized as statist model. This period is also described as an "era of command and control" due to stringent legal rules and regulations to govern the activities of the private sector (Ray and Ray 2012). High taxes and license system imposed restrictions on the private sector which indirectly triggered corporate malpractices at the same time. Labour and environmental standards became face of the political agenda and the subject of legislation. Despite the progressive nature of economy where businesses were to play their part as respectable corporate citizens, and engage into regular stakeholder dialogues, social accountability and transparency the Statist approach did not materialize at that time and corporate philanthropy was still practiced (Mohan 2001).

4.2.4 Liberal Approach (1980–1990)

During 1980s traditional engagement of CSR as corporate philanthropy was being abandoned by Indian companies and CSR was integrated into as a sustainable business strategy. During 1990s, the Indian economy was liberalized and deregulated to overcome the shortcomings of the mixed economy and to integrate India into the global market. During liberalisation reforms controls and license systems were partly abolished, and rapid growth was pronounced in the economy. The trend towards liberalization and privatization led to deregulation making companies solely responsible to owners characterize third model of corporate social responsibility viz liberal model. Along with this rapid growth there was a further increase in the philanthropic donations commensurate with the increased profitability and enhanced expectations from business from public in general and government (Arora and Puranik 2004; Chahoud et al. 2007).

The liberal model is consistent with doctrine by Milton Friedman (1970), who challenged the very notion of corporate responsibility for anything other than part of profit maximisation decision.

4.2.5 Stakeholder Approach (After 1991)

Since 1990s globally trend of CSR has emerged which is beyond charity and philanthropy. Under the doctrine of Stakeholder Theory (Freeman 1984) CSR has evolved as corporate strategy which is closely related to core business. The stakeholder approach is further propagated by management scientists such as Peter

Drucker and many other authors as a part of corporate strategy emphasizing that survival of the corporation depends on not only the responsibility towards shareholders but also towards employees, governments, customers and community in general.[5] As a result of globalization and liberalization that integrated Indian economy into world economy there has been a fundamental transformation from charitable donations at individual levels to integrating community in organisation's reputation and success. The aforementioned transformation occurred as the outsourcing of production and manufacturing units flourished in India and Indian corporates started following labour and environmental standards imposed on them by their western counterparts. Market competition among Indian exporters influenced more and more compliance with the International standards related to CSR and corporate governance.

4.3 Principles and Guidelines on Corporate Social Responsibility in India

This section presents principles and guidelines governing CSR in India and provides a comparison with the international standards.

4.3.1 Guidelines on Social, Environmental and Economic Responsibilities of Business

The Directorate of Public Enterprises (DPE) formalized CSR for PSUs in 2010 which was further formulated as National Voluntary Guidelines (NVGs) for the "Social, Environmental and Economic Responsibilities of Business" in 2011 by the Ministry of Corporate Affairs (MCA) in 2011. DPE guidelines views CSR in a different perspective based on triple P Model—People, Planet, and Profit—all the stakeholders are engaged for a common good and CSR demonstrates the business process and commitment which is organizationally embedded. More formally DPE guidelines are revised after enactment of the Companies Act 2013 which integrates CSR and Sustainability as a company's commitment to its stakeholders to conduct business in an Economically, Socially and Environmentally sustainable manner that is transparent and ethical. Under the revised guidelines the

[5]For example According to Peter Drucker, "Leaders in every single institution and in every single sector … have two responsibilities. They are responsible and accountable for the performance of their institutions, and that requires them and their institutions to be concentrated, focused, limited. They are responsible also, however, for the community as a whole.".

allocation of CSR and sustainability activities is emphasized along with a mandate for Central PSUs (CPSEs) to take up at least one major project for developing a backward district. The underlying aim is towards contributing in the long run socio-economic growth of backward regions of the country. The revised guidelines outline the activities that can be defined as CSR and sustainability as:

- Capacity building,
- Empowerment of communities,
- Inclusive socio-economic growth,
- Environment protection,
- Promotion of green and energy efficient technologies,
- Development of backward regions, and upliftment of the marginalised and under- privileged sections of the society.

Compared to DPE guidelines NVG guidelines are not prescriptive in nature. NVGs are aimed to advise socially responsibly conduct for Indian businesses by outlining nine principles which are based on realities of Indian business environment and society adapted to the global trends. Specifically these principles are related to (1) ethics and transparency, (2) product life cycle sustainability, (3) employee well-being, (4) stakeholder engagement, (5) human rights, (6) environmental stewardship, (7) responsible policy advocacy, (8) inclusive development and (9) consumer well-being respectively elaborated as follows:

(i) *conduct and govern themselves with ethics, transparency and accountability*
(ii) *provide goods and services that are safe and contribute to sustainability throughout their life cycle*
(iii) *promote the wellbeing of all employees*
(iv) *respect the interests of, and be responsive towards all stakeholders, especially those who are disadvantaged, vulnerable and marginalised*
(v) *respect and promote human rights*
(vi) *respect, protect, and make efforts to restore the environment*
(vii) *when engaged in influencing public and regulatory policy, do so in a responsible manner*
(viii) *support inclusive growth and equitable development*
(ix) *engage with and provide value to their customers and consumers in a responsible manner.*

While the TBL approach is urged for the businesses, NVGs guide businesses to harmonize the interface of financial performance with the expectations of society, environment, people and society at large in a sustainable manner.

DPE guidelines also mention that CPSEs are expected to adhere to the global standards such as the UN Global Compact and the UN Business and the Millennium Development Goals (BDGs) to strengthen responsible business initiatives which are described in the previous section.

4.3.2 Global Compact Society in India

Global Compact Society (GCS) is an Indian forum of organisations participating in the UN Global Compact. The GCS undertakes a number of activities to create awareness and to assist GC participants in India to internalize the UN Global Compact ten principles. GCS further helps Indian organizations to exchange experiences, network and work together on activities related to CSR.[6]

4.3.3 The Responsible Entrepreneurs Achievement Programme (REAP)

REAP was developed by United Nations Industrial Development Organization (UNIDO) formalizing CSR based management and reporting tool for SMEs in developing countries to implement CSR concepts that will align economic, social and environmental aspects of business underlying the concept of TBL. Based on the ten principles of the UN Global Compact, as well as international standards in the social and environmental domains, such as ISO 14001, SA 8000, or OHSAS 18001, it provides a structured framework in combination with an analytical software, which can be used to gather, process, evaluate and report data to track progress in implementing CSR in SMEs.

Social accountability 8000 (SA8000) launched by Social Accountability International as a voluntary accountability standard for workplaces based on International Organisation and United Nations conventions has over 300,000 individuals employed in 458 SA8000 certified facilities throughout India.

4.4 CSR Provisions in the Companies Act 2013

The Companies Act, 1956, was enacted to amend and consolidate the Company Law relating to companies and certain other associations following the recommendations of the Bhaba Committe in 1950. The Companies Act, 1956, has been amended as many as 24 times since 1956 with major amendments in 1988 and 2002 respectively. The 2013 Act recommends several changes in the way companies operate and mechanisms to regulate the functions of the corporate in a transparent manner. Though the corporate sector formally engaged itself with the CSR in 1960s, the Companies Act 1956 did not include any formal rules to regulate

[6]The Confederation of Indian Industry (CII) and the Global Compact entered into a Memorandum of Understanding in 2007 whereby the CII formally pledged to build the capacity of corporations operating in India and around the world to implement the principles of the Global Compact within their business operations.

this engagement. The first set of guidelines was introduced by MCA in December 2009 which was further formalized in the form of DPE and NVG guidelines in 2010 and 2011 respectively. These guidelines formally signalled government's intentions to involve the corporate sector in the development of the country and focused on the process of 'cradle-to-grave' in the life cycle of products and services. At the same time the guidelines formally linked corporate governance and social responsibility by realizing that responsible business practices should be achieved through conscientious corporate governance.

Providing a framework for companies to implement need-based CSR activities, the Government of India included CSR-related provisions in the Companies Bill, 2012 which was further notified by the MCA on 27th February, 2014 as Section 135 in the new Companies Act, 2013 effective from 1st April, 2014. The new Companies Act 2013 mandates the CSR spending up to 2 % of the average net profit as responsibility of companies that meet certain criteria. Though a clear definition of CSR in not provided in the Act, the appertaining Rules to Clause 135 describe CSR as: "… the process by which an organization thinks about and evolves its relationships with stakeholders for the common good, and demonstrates its commitment in this regard by adoption of appropriate business processes and strategies, thus CSR is not charity or mere donations".

The Act outlines the economic conditions for the corporations who are required to allocate two percent of their preceding three years Profit After Tax (PAT). Specifically, the requirement applies to any registered company that is incorporated in India, whether domestic or subsidiary to a foreign company, and which meets one or more of these conditions during any financial year.

- Turnover of Rs. 1000 Crore[7] or more or
- Net worth of Rs. 500 Crore or more, or
- Net profit of Rs. 5 Crore or more

Companies meeting any of the above criteria are required to constitute a CSR Committee consisting of three or more directors, out of which at least one director should be an independent director. Further Clause 135 outlines guidelines related to CSR activities and responsibilities of the CSR committee are listed below:

1. The Board's report under sub-section (3) of section 134 shall disclose the composition of the Corporate Social Responsibility Committee.
2. The responsibilities of CSR Committee are
   (a) formulate and recommend to the Board, a Corporate Social Responsibility Policy which shall indicate the activities to be undertaken by the company as specified in Schedule VII;
   (b) recommend the amount of expenditure to be incurred on the activities referred to in clause (a); and
   (c) monitor the Corporate Social Responsibility Policy of the company from time to time.

[7]"Crore" is a unit in the Indian numbering system equal to ten million.

3. The Board of every company referred to in sub-section (1) shall
   (a) after taking into account the recommendations made by the Corporate Social Responsibility Committee, approve the Corporate Social Responsibility Policy for the company and disclose contents of such Policy in its report and also place it on the company's website, if any, in such manner as may be prescribed; and
   (b) ensure that the activities as are included in Corporate Social Responsibility Policy of the company are undertaken by the company
4. The Board of every company referred to in sub-section (1), shall ensure that the company spends, in every financial year, at least two per cent of the average net profits of the company made during the three immediately preceding financial years, in pursuance of its CSR Policy:

Further the Act requires that if the company fails to spend on CSR, the Board should explain the reasons for not spending the amount in the board's report as per Clause (o) of sub-section (3) of section 134. In addition to the provisions to formulate and regulate the CSR activities, the Companies Act, 2013 introduced disclose-or-explain of CSR activities. For this purpose, Clause (135) and Schedule VII suggesting a list of CSR activities are included in the Act as follows:

- Eradicating extreme hunger and poverty;
- Promotion of education;
- Promoting gender equality and empowering women;
- Reducing child mortality and improving maternal health;
- Combating human immunodeficiency virus, acquired immuned efficiency syndrome, malaria and other diseases;
- Ensuring environmental sustainability;
- Employment-enhancing vocational skills;
- Social business projects;
- Contribution to the Prime Minister's National Relief Fund or any other fund set up by the Central Government or the state governments for socio-economic development, and relief and funds for the welfare of the Scheduled Castes, the Scheduled Tribes, other backward classes, minorities and women;
- Such other matters as may be prescribed.

The Act allows various methods in which companies can engage into CSR activities as follows. CSR can be practiced directly by company by donating funds to charitable institutions such as UNICEF, Red Cross; by setting up non-profit foundation; by hiring agencies/Non-governmental Organisations (NGOs); or collaborating with other companies to pool resources to carry out CSR activities/projects. Some of the companies have existing administrative machinery and staff to perform the CSR activities.[8]

[8]For example Tata motors have a separate CSR Committee comprising the Managing Director and the Senior Management which meets from time to time to fulfil the community and social responsibilities of its stakeholders. Similarly GMR has its own GMR Varalakshmi Foundation (GMRVF) that implements local specific, need-based interventions to improve the quality of

In addition to the prescription of CSR committee, its responsibilities and the schedule of CSR activities, the distinguishing features of the Act include that only CSR activities undertaken in India will be taken into consideration; activities meant exclusively for employees and their families will not qualify under the Act. Another distinguishing feature of the Act is an explicit format for the board report on detailed CSR activities demonstrating compliance with CSR objectives signed by the CEO/MD/Director. In case of non-compliance, the board should include an explanation in its responsibility statement. The comply-or-explain approach is similar to that was followed in the corporate governance report of Clause 49 which was mandated eventually since 2005.

Finally, in the next section, we summarize the existing studies that focus on Indian studies. We divide the section into three subsections to describe general studies, empirical studies and case studies respectively.

4.5 Corporate Social Responsibility in India—Review of Literature

Literature on the empirical analysis of CSR in Indian companies is evolving mostly due to limited availability of quantifiable information from annual reports. We review the existing literature focusing on three types of studies. First we summarize various studies based on general observations on development of CSR in India. Secondly, we review specific case studies and finally we summarize empirical or large sample studies.

4.5.1 General Studies on Corporate Social Responsibility

These studies can be divided among comparative studies comparing India with other countries as well as standalone studies on India about the perception of CSR and its impact on firm valuation. Cultural aspect of CSR is explored in a study by Khan and Atkinson (1987) by analysing and provides a comparison of the

Footnote 8 (continued)

lives of the target communities focusing on three thrust areas viz. education; health, hygiene and sanitation; empowerment and livelihood respectively. Cairn India committed itself to the United Nations Millennium Development Goals and the GOI's vision of fostering inclusive growth, as articulated in the Eleventh Five Year Plan and the Approach Paper to the Twelfth Five Year Plan. Polaris software's CSR initiatives through Ullas Trust is an employee oriented initiative to integrate Polaris with a larger community and enable them to enjoy the bliss of working with young minds in the country. The primary motive of Ullas is to recognize academic excellence in students from the economically challenged sections of our society and encourage the "Can do" spirit towards chasing their dreams and aspirations.

executive perception on the CSR in UK and India. The paper also presents organisational similarities, differences, management's involvement in social action programmes, and problems of implementing and monitoring Social Responsibility in two countries. The study finds that a large percentage of Indian executives accept that CSR is relevant to business and support the notion of business's responsibility not only to the shareholders and employees but also to customers, suppliers, society and the state in general. Focusing on the perceptions of consumers about CSR, Gupta (2011) analyses the similarities and differences in CSR perception of consumers in India and America respectively. Using a web-based questionnaire the author reports that there is a substantial unawareness in US consumers about CSR initiatives compared to their Indian counterparts who are unaware of CSR initiatives of multinational corporations. Finally, comparing the valuation effects of CSR in Asia, Cheung et al. (2010) investigates whether firm value increases for 1118 firms in nine countries (China, Hong Kong, India, Indonesia, Korea, Malaysia, Singapore, Taiwan and Thailand) that engage in CSR. The study finds significant association between CSR and market valuation of these firms between sample period 2001–2004.

Analysing perception of CSR, Balasubramanian et al. (2005) presents CSR perceptions of the urban, young managerial community in India. Based on a survey conducted by Center for Corporate Governance and Citizenship in 2001, the paper presents case-based research findings on CSR initiatives by two new IT corporations' CSR initiatives and concludes that CSR developments affect strategic planning suggesting India may establish a unique position where CSR becomes a driving force for change. Further to explore drivers and barriers to implementing CSR practices Arevalo and Aravind (2011) analyze the ethical, the statist, the liberal, and the stakeholder approach. Based on a survey of top-level managers of a sample of companies engaging in a CSR initiative across a variety of industry sectors Arevalo and Aravind (2011) finds that the stakeholder approach is the most favoured CSR approach in Indian firms and the drivers for this approach are primarily moral followed by strategic. Further, the authors suggest that the most significant barriers to CSR implementation are those related to lack of resources, followed by those related to the complexity and difficulty of implementing CSR.

Ahmed (2009) empirical analysed 300 Indian companies which are active in 26 various theme areas for their CSR initiatives. Her research results showed that community welfare perceived to be the top priority area on the corporate sector's list with a share of 22 % out of the total 26 activities. It involves activities that focus more towards the underprivileged community that lives around the vicinity of company plants, facilitating education and health care and supporting projects that lead to employment generation. The second most important CSR initiative is providing education and enlightening the youth of the country is the focus of Indian companies.

To understand the state of reporting of sustainability initiatives in India Jose and Saraf (2013) analyze India's top 100 companies which are most valued by shareholders. Using data from companies' websites and annual reports for the second quarter of 2011, the authors find that the information reported is highest for corporate governance, followed by CSR initiatives and measures to improve operational efficiency. Where reporting on corporate governance is consistent with the reforms, CSR reporting is voluntary in nature and provides the current status of organisational commitment. The study reveals that CSR initiatives mainly focused on four areas viz education, healthcare, community livelihood, and infrastructure development respectively. Also interesting to note is that disclosures on CSR finances and donations were also nearly non-existent. We also observe this problem in our dataset of largest 500 companies and devise methodology to overcome this problem of non-reporting which does not necessarily means lack of CSR activity.

4.5.2 Case Studies on CSR in India

This section presents selective case studies to highlight existing CSR practices and organisational commitment followed by some of the companies in India. Bruche (2010) conducts case study of Tata Motors to explore effect of group-affiliation on value-creation, leadership, ethics and sustainable development given the backdrop of rapid internationalization through resource acquisition thereby shifting stakeholders' expectations for corporate social responsibility. In a focused case study on Tata Group, Srivastava et al. (2012) explores the rise of business group beyond notion of profitability and caring for all those associated with their survival in the society directly or indirectly. This study delves into an understanding about the CSR practiced by TATA Group who exemplified and pioneered the sense of responsibility towards the upliftment of common masses and protection of the environment and development of the nation. Given the fact that Tata group is one of the largest, oldest and diversified business groups in India that operates more than 80 companies employing around 200,000 employees across various industries ranging from steel, automobiles and software to consumer goods and telecommunications the study reports in depth about the initiatives and programs running under various companies under the umbrella of Tata Group. More importantly this case study demonstrates that the CSR is being practiced not only at the consolidated level but every affiliated company engages into responsibility initiatives.

More recently Srivastava and Goyal (2015) provide a case study on Mahindra and Mahindra group which is another organisation engaging actively into CSR practices. The group has ongoing scholarship and grant programmes like "Nanhi Kali" as well as disaster relief and rehabilitation, Employee Social Options (ESOPs), Lifeline express etc. More recently, the organisation committed to dedicate 1 % of its PAT towards CSR. During 2011–12, the organisation made an investment of Rs. 720 million on CSR initiatives which is an increase of 42 % over the last fiscal. The organisation runs distinguishing programmes like "ESOPs" that enable Mahindra workforce to collectively donate thousands of human hours for various social projects in the three focused areas of education, health and environment, making social work an integral part of their lives.

4.5.3 Empirical Studies on CSR in India

Sahoo and Nayak (2008) explores the importance of Green Banking which has not been initiated by the banks and other financial institutions in India. The study argues that environmental impact might affect the quality of assets and also rate of return of banks in the long-run and therefore the banks should play a pro-active role to take environmental and ecological aspects as part of their lending principle, which would force industries to go for mandated investment for environmental management, use of appropriate technologies and management systems. Using an empirical framework and sample of 30 commercial banks in India Sharma and Mani (2013) analyze the CSR activities carried out by these banks during 20010–2012. The study includes variables such as rural branch expansion, priority sector lending, environment protection, community welfare, women welfare, new initiative related to CSR, financial literacy, education and farmers' welfare to capture CSR initiatives and find that the public sector banks have overall highest contribution in CSR activities. Private sector banks and foreign banks are clearly lagging. By mapping the CSR practices of large banks Bihari and Pradhan (2011) find the positive impact of CSR on the performance and image of the bank in general. In a recent study to understand specific CSR initiatives of nationalized Indian banks Moharana (2013) finds that selected banks (Allahabad Bank, Andhra Bank, Bank of Baroda, State Bank of India, and UCO Bank) are directly engaged in CSR activities mostly in the area of Rural Development, Education, Community Welfare, Women and Children. Her analysis shows that despite the greater efforts for implementing CSR, there exist barriers in certain fields which can be eliminated by adding the formal link of social development issues in the corporate sector to which the banks are lending. This is similar to the notion of Green Banking (Sahoo and Nayak 2008).

Using a more diversified sample of Nifty 50 companies that includes firms from manufacturing, banking and other industries, Anees (2012) find that CSR initiatives are independent of all the companies' profitability level, their ownership status and the type of their business activities i.e., service or manufacturing in general. This is in line with Kumar (2012) which finds using 30 BSE listed companies that CSR initiatives of the companies under study are independent of the level of revenue, type of ownership and the type of public and private sector. Due to lack of reporting initiatives with regard to CSR, many authors use the questionnaire approach. For example, Mishra and Suar (2010) collect perceptual data on CSR from 150 senior-level Indian managers including CEOs through questionnaire survey and analyze whether CSR towards primary stakeholders influences the financial (FP) and the non-financial performance (NFP) of Indian firms. The authors construct a composite measure of CSR by aggregating the six dimensions capturing stakeholder groups along which the questionnaire is developed namely—employees, customers, investors, community, natural environment, and suppliers. Findings by Mishra and Suar (2010) indicate that listed firms show responsible business practices correlated with better FP than unlisted firms. Also, after controlling for effects of listing, ownership, and firm size, positive perception of managers towards CSR is associated with increase in FP and NFP of sample firms. Their findings are robust for CSR assessment for the six stakeholder groups in aggregate as well as separately for each stakeholder group. Therefore, Mishra and Suar (2010) suggest that responsible business practices towards primary stakeholders can be profitable and beneficial to Indian firms in general.

The positive link between CSR and financial performance is well established in the literature across most of the countries including India (for example see Harpreet 2009). The factors which affect this association are conceptually formalized as management's ability to incorporate CSR as a corporate strategy. The empirical support to this hypothesis is provided by Sangle (2010) who finds that ability to integrate CSR with other functional strategies is the most critical success factor for CSR. Using data on Indian public sector organisations Sangle (2010) further reports that other critical success factors are ability to manage stakeholder groups, ability to evaluate benefits of CSR and top management support respectively. With respect to specific CSR initiatives large sample studies are very limited in India. For example, Pradhan and Ranjan (2010) analyze the impact of CSR actions on the socio-economic development of rural people as stakeholders using web-based information on fourteen public and private Indian companies who have undertaken CSR practices specific to rural development. Similar to other large sample studies Pradhan and Ranjan (2010) corroborate that social responsibility is independent of size, sector, and business goal and impact positively not only on the development of rural community but also on their businesses.

In the context of new CSR guidelines applicable for public sector companies Ray (2012) investigates the relation between CSR and sustainable development and barriers to operationalize and implement CSR projects. Using interviews of 50 managers in the backdrop of NVGs and DPE guidelines Ray (2012) reports that potential barriers are engagement, institutional mechanisms, capacity building and knowledge management respectively. Further, Deva (2012) critically examines whether the Indian initiatives—the National Voluntary Guidelines on Social, Environmental and Economic Responsibilities of Business 2011 and the Companies Bill 2011—have a distinctly Indian identity, as claimed by the government. The author further argues that an Indian approach to CSR as "trusteeship" may fail to work in an era where companies operate globally and the TBL as 'core' of socially responsible business is fast becoming a commonly accepted currency at international level.

Based on reporting initiatives of top 200 listed Indian companies Singh and Agarwal (2013) highlight that predominant categories of CSR disclosure is Education, Health, Community Welfare, Entrepreneurship Development, Environment, Market Place, and Rural Development respectively. The study also highlights the way in which companies engage into these CSR activities. Most of the CSR activities are undertaken through NGOs or other charitable organisations (62 out of 200), followed by collaborating with government agencies (46 out of 200). Further the results reveal scope of outreach with most of the companies engage with local communities near their area of operations, and the beneficiaries of CSR activities are generally the local population.

Karmayog is the first organization in India that compiles CSR ranking for 1000 selected Indian companies between 2007 and 2011 based on disclosure of CSR initiatives and amount spent. The study also captures the CSR initiatives and reporting across different ownership structures (government owned, private, multinational); operating industries; global and local conditions that demand more responsible behaviour by all stakeholders respectively. Providing a status report on where Indian companies stand in terms of actual CSR spending given the mandatory requirements in the Companies Act 2013, a study conducted by Forbes provided a CSR Report Card for top 100 Indian companies using information collected from standalone annual reports for the financial year 2012. The study reports that about 52 % of the companies reported the actual CSR spending out of which 6 companies incur more than 2 % of three years average PAT. Further, large business houses such as Reliance, Tata, and Jindal are among the top spenders on the CSR activates along with the central public enterprises such as Oil and Natural Gas Corporation, Coal India, Indian Oil Corporation, and State Bank of India. Similar to Forbes, Socio Research & Reform Foundation (SRRF) analyse the CSR spending of top Indian companies using their annual reports of two years viz 2011–12 and 2012–13. The findings of the study reveal marginal increase from Forbes study that about 57 companies reported CSR spending and banking sector is leading in terms of contributions during the year 2012–13. A notable difference between Forbes and SRRF is that Forbes is based on CSR spending and donations from the standalone annual reports whereas SRRF is based on the consolidated annual reports for the firms affiliated to the business groups. Therefore SRRF captures the CSR spending at the group level. This is important as the Companies Act 2013 does not explicitly mention about the CSR activities undertaken by the group parent company which may be unlisted entity. In our analysis we also collect the relevant information from both the standalone and consolidated audited statements to acquire a better understanding on the patterns of expenses made for social responsibility particularly by the group companies.

4.6 Conclusion

The concept of social responsibility in business is not new in India. The country has a long tradition of corporate philanthropy and industrial welfare that has been put in practice since as long as 1800s. Business is known for not only creating excess wealth for its own, but also creates social and environmental concerns that are deep roots in the history of business in India (Gautam and Singh 2010). Particularly in number of family-based organisations, traditionally it has been set with a strong community ethos (Chendroyaperumal and Juliet 2009).

This chapter elaborates the historical evolution of Corporate Social Responsibility in a phased manner along with the insights on pre and post industrialisation and globalisation scenario in India. The chapter also presents the recent guidelines to conduct CSR related activities including the recent changes in the Companies Act 2013 formalizing the CSR activities among large Indian companies.

Further the chapter provides a comprehensive literature survey of studies including generic studies, case studies and large sample studies exploring the impact of CSR which creates the necessary backdrop for our empirical framework for analysing the nature of CSR spending and the motivation behind undertaking these initiatives by large Indian companies.

References

Ahmed N (2009) ASSOCHAM eco pulse study: corporate social responsibility 2008-09. ASSOCHAM research bureau

Anees M (2012) Corporate social responsibility in india based on NSE NIFTY companies. Int J Market Financ Ser Manage Res 1(12): 70–79

Arevalo JA, Aravind D (2011) Corporate social responsibility practices in India: approach, drivers, and barriers", Corporate Govern 11(4):399–414

Arora B, Puranik R (2004) A review of corporate social responsibility in india. Development 47(3):93–100

Balasubramanian NK, Kimber D, Siemensma F (2005) Emerging opportunities or traditions reinforced. J Corporate Citizenship 2005(17):79–92

Bihari SC, Pradhan S (2011) CSR and Performance: The story of banks in India. J Trans Manage 16(1):20–35

Bruche G (2010) Tata motor's transformational resource acquisition path: a case study of latecomer catch-up in a business group context (no. 55). Working papers of the institute of management berlin at the berlin school of economics and law (HWR Berlin)

Chahoud T, Emmerling J, Kolb D, Kubina I, Repinski G (2007) Corporate social and environmental responsibility in india-assessing the UN global compac's role

Chendroyaperumal C, Juliet A (2009) Corporate Social Responsibility: Modern and Indian Views, Emerg Mark: Econ e -Jour 2(70). Available at SSRN: http://ssrn.com/abstract=1335137

Cheung Y-L, Tan W, Ahn H-J, Zhang Z (2010) Does corporate social responsibility matter in Asian emerging markets? J Bus Ethics 92(3):401–413

Deva S (2012) Socially responsible business in india: has the elephant finally woken up to the tunes of international trends? Common Law World Rev 41:299–321

Flash Eurobarometer (2013) How companies influence our society: citizens' view, report. European commission. Available on http://ec.europa.eu/public_opinion/flash/fl_363_en.pdf. Accessed 09 July 2013

Freeman RE (1984) Strategic management: a stakeholder approach. Pitman, Boston

Friedman M (1970) The social responsibility of business is to increase profits, N Y Times Mag 32–33:122–126

Gautam R, Singh A (2010) Corporate social responsibility practices in india: a study of top 500 companies. Global Bus Manage Res: Int J 2(1):41–56

Gopinath C (2005) Trusteeship as a moral foundation for business. Bus Soc Rev 110:331–344

Gupta Das A (2007) Social responsibility in India towards global compact approach. Int J Soc Eco 34(9):637–663

Gupta S (2011) Consumer stakeholder view of corporate social responsibility: a comparative analysis from USA and India. Soc Responsib J 7(3):363–380

Gupta AD (2012) Corporate social responsibility and strategy a bird's eye view. Global Bus Rev 13(1):153–165
Harpreet SB (2009) Financial performance and social responsibility: indian scenerio, http://ssrn.com/abstract=1496291
IPSOS-Mori (2013) CSR market assessment: quantitative stage report. Retrieved from http://www.unicef.org.uk/Documents/Media/CSR%20Market%20Assessment.pdf
Jose PD, Saraf S (2013) Corporate sustainability initiatives reporting: a study of india's most valuable companies. IIM bangalore research paper (428)
Khan AF, Atkinson A (1987) Managerial attitudes to social responsibility: a comparative study in India and Britain, J Bus Ethics 6:419–432
Kumar S (2012) Application of chi square to analyse corporate social responsibility: A Study of BSE Sensex (30) based Companies, J IPEM 6(1):1–11
Kumar NS, Rao US (1996) Guidelines for value based management in Kautilya's Arthashastra. J Bus Ethics 15(4):415–423
Kumar R, Murphy DF, Mortier R, Rathnasiri C, Gunaratne L (2004) Understanding and encouraging corporate responsibility in South Asia, Update two: Sri Lanka, TERI Press, New Delhi
Masani RP (1956) The role of wealth in society. Bombay, The Popular Book Depot, India
Mishra S, Suar D (2010) Social responsibility. Soc Responsib J 6(2):306–327
Mohan A (2001) Corporate Citizenship: Perspectives from India. J Corp Citizen 2:107–117
Moharana S (2013) Corporate social responsibility: a study of selected public sector banks in india, IOSR J Bus Manage (IOSR-JBM) 15(4):01–09
Narayan J (1966) Social responsibility of business. Manaktalas, Bombay
Nielsen (2012) Global corporate social responsibility report. Retrieved from http://www.nielsen.com/content/dam/nielsenglobal/apac/docs/reports/2014/Nielsen-Global-Corporate-Social-Responsibility-Report-June-2014.pdf
Pachauri RK (2004) The rationale for corporate social responsibility in India. Financ Express 22
Pradhan S, Ranjan A (2010) Corporate social responsibility in rural development sector: evidences from india. School Doctoral Stud (European Union) J pp 139–147
Ray S (2012) Corporate Social responsibility, resettlement, rehabilitation and community involvement in india. Reg Insights 3(1):15–17
Ray DS, Ray IA (2012) A Close Look into Corporate Social Responsibility in India. World Science Publisher, United States Advances in Asian Social Science 2(3):479–488
Renold L (1994) Gandhi: Patron saint of the industrialist. South Asia Grad Res J, Introd Issue 1(1)
Sahoo P, Nayak B (2008) Green banking in india, Discussion paper series No. 125, Institute of Economic Growth, University of Delhi
Sangle S (2010) Critical success factors for corporate social responsibility: a public sector perspective. Corp Soc Resp Env Manage 17(4):205–214
Sen SK, Bhattacharya A, Das SK (1999) A selective location update strategy for PCS users. Wirel Networks 5(5): 313–326
Sharma E, Mani M (2013) Corporate social responsibility: an analysis of Indian commercial banks. AIMA J Manage Res 7(1/4). ISSN 0974-497
Singh R, Agarwal S (2013) Corporate social responsibility for social impact: approach to measure social impact using CSR impact index, Indian Institute of Management Calcutta,Working Paper (June 2013)
Sood A, Arora B (2006) The political economy of corporate responsibility in India: Examining the nature of CSR in India. UNRISD 18
Srivastava P, Goyal S (2015) The Pre and Post legislative development of CSR in India: A case illustration of Mahindra and Mahindra . Asian J Manage Res. ISSN 2229-3795
Srivastava A, Negi G, Mishra V, Pandey S (2012) Corporate social responsibility: a case study of TATA group. J Bus Manage 3(5):17–27
Sundar P (2000) Beyond business: from merchant charity to corporate citizenship. Tata mac graw hill, New Delhi

Chapter 5
Corporate Governance: An Overview

5.1 Introduction

This chapter presents the background in the concepts and mechanisms of corporate governance and provides the state of corporate governance mechanisms in India.

The basis of corporate governance is a classical principal-agent problem. Investors are 'principals' who provide funds (debt or equity) to set up a company and delegate the day to day management of the company to professional managers as 'agents'. While this separation of ownership from control has obvious benefits, for instance, by allowing finance and investment decisions to be managed by professionals with specialized talents, it also creates a potential for agency conflict. This separation of ownership from control generates agency costs which are associated with: (1) writing complete contracts defining accountability and responsibility of managers, (2) asymmetric information (managers being better informed about the company performance and future prospects), and (3) monitoring the managerial efforts.[1] Agency costs ultimately result in the suboptimal firm performance and the suppliers of finance are forced to bear the delta. Corporate governance is therefore a set of mechanisms to solve the agency problem by: (1) providing managers with proper incentives to induce them to work for value maximization and thereby aligning their interests with those of suppliers of finance and, (2) making managers accountable to firm performance. As theoretical and empirical literature has developed over the years into both firm-level as well as cross country, these mechanisms are both company as well as country based. In other

[1]This theory of ownership structure in the modern corporation was developed by Jensen and Meckling (1976). These economists formalized the basic idea of conflicts of interest between managers and owners that dates back to Smith (1776): "The directors of such [joint-stock] companies, however, being the managers rather of other people's money than of their own, it cannot well be expected, that they should watch over it with the same anxious vigilance with which the partners in a private co-partnery frequently watch over their own." Since then, other theories of corporate governance are developed in other subjects of economics. See Hart (1980) for transaction cost economics and Tirole (2001) for law and economics frameworks.

S.N. Bhaduri and E. Selarka, *Corporate Governance and Corporate Social Responsibility of Indian Companies*, CSR, Sustainability, Ethics & Governance,
DOI 10.1007/978-981-10-0925-9_5

words, corporate governance is a set of institutional and market-based instruments that induce the self-interested controllers of a company to make decisions that maximize the value of the company to its owners (Denis and McConnell 2003).[2]

Why corporate governance has become important? Over the last decade corporate governance has become a key concern of not only economists but also of regulators, corporations, and policy and law makers around the world. Two historical events have played a dominant role in portraying the effect of bad corporate governance at firm level: (1) the 1998 emerging market crises in Asia, Russia and Brazil when deficiencies and expropriation in corporate sector affected the financial stability of these economies, and (2) three years later, industrial economies witnessed a variety of corporate scandals highlighting issues like corporate collapses (Enron), managerial corporate looting (Tyco), and fraudulent audit (Arthur Anderson) to undue profit boosting (Worldcomm). These events triggered the realization of bad corporate governance at company level on overall financial health of the country and led to the reforms of corporate governance in developed as well as developing and emerging countries.

The importance of good corporate governance at the company, market and country level and its relevance with overall development of country has been well established in the literature.[3] There are two main channels for implementing good corporate governance: (1) by limiting expropriation by controlling shareholders/managers, and (2) by better monitoring of management. Both theoretical and empirical literatures support these two channels and it is well established that corporate governance practices play a crucial role in efficient company functioning and shareholder protection and are consequently reflected in positive company valuation (see Shliefer and Vishny 1997; Denis and McConnell 2003; Claessens 2006 for comprehensive surveys on the subject).

[2]A survey of the literature on corporate governance reveals a wide array of definitions of corporate governance. From a corporate finance perspective, corporate governance deals with the ways in which suppliers of finance to corporations, i.e., debt-holders and equity-holders, exercise control and ensure accountability of company management so as to assure themselves of getting the best possible return on their investment (Shleifer and Vishny 1997). From a law and economics perspective, corporate governance refers to the defense of shareholders' interests (Tirole 2001). A policy perspective is that, corporate governance is the system by which companies are directed and controlled (Cadbury 1992). In other words, corporate governance refers to the legal rules, institutional arrangements and practices that determine who controls business corporations, and who gets the benefits that flow from them (Blair 1995).

[3]See Claessens (2006) for the most recent survey of literature on corporate governance and development. The literature that establishes the link between effective corporate governance and economic development includes two types of studies: (1) first type of studies show that country level governance characteristics like investor protection, enforcement etc. are associated with various development variables, (2) second type of studies find a relationship between country-based governance elements and financial performance of firms after controlling for cross country differences. Seminal works of LaPorta et al. (1997, 1998, 2000) show that higher investor protection at country level is associated with greater access to finance, more capital market development and higher company valuation. Claessens (2006)—shows that effective corporate governance system irrespective of type of external financing—bank or equity—promote development of strong financial systems which in turn lead to economic growth and well being.

Along with the industrial and corporate sector reforms, corporate governance reforms have been instituted in the country to enforce disclosure and regulation of internal and external governance mechanisms for the listed firms. On one hand, restructuring of internal mechanisms will invoke what is called "self discipline" in corporations and at the same time, external mechanisms will provide the market discipline. In this context, our empirical work incorporates these mechanisms and analyze their relevance and effectiveness for CSR expenditure. In the next section we present a general background on corporate governance mechanisms. Finally, Sect. 5.3 briefly discusses the corporate governance background in India.

5.2 Corporate Governance Mechanisms

Figure 5.1 presents a framework of corporate governance mechanisms. Governance mechanisms are broadly categorized into being internal and external to the firm. Internal mechanisms that gained primary interest in the literature are ownership structure, board of directors, capital structure, and compensation policies. The primary external mechanisms are market for corporate control and legal/ regulatory system at country level.[4]

5.2.1 Internal Corporate Governance Mechanisms

A. **Ownership Structure**

Ownership structure is defined by the distribution of equity with regard to votes and capital but also by the identity of the equity owners. These structures are of major importance in corporate governance because they affect the incentives of managers and thereby the efficiency of the firm. Therefore, the relation between ownership and company value has received much attention in the literature. Early research on corporate governance was based on the assumption of widely held ownership structure where owners are dispersed and managers have control over corporate decisions. Recent line of research shows that ownership is concentrated even in largest American corporations (Demsetz and Lehn 1985a; Shleifer and Vishny 1986a; Morck et al. 1988), and widely held corporation is an exception rather than a rule in other developed and developing countries (LaPorta et al. 1998, 1999). On one hand, large shareholders mitigate free-rider problems of corporate

[4]There are numerous surveys written addressing these mechanisms. To name a few See John and Senbet (1998) and Hermalin and Weisbach (2002) on boards of directors, Core et al. (2003) and Murphy (1999) on executive compensation, Holderness (2002) on blockholders, Holmstrom and Kaplan (2001) on merger activity, and Karpoff (1998) on shareholder activism, Harris and Raviv (1988) on capital structure.

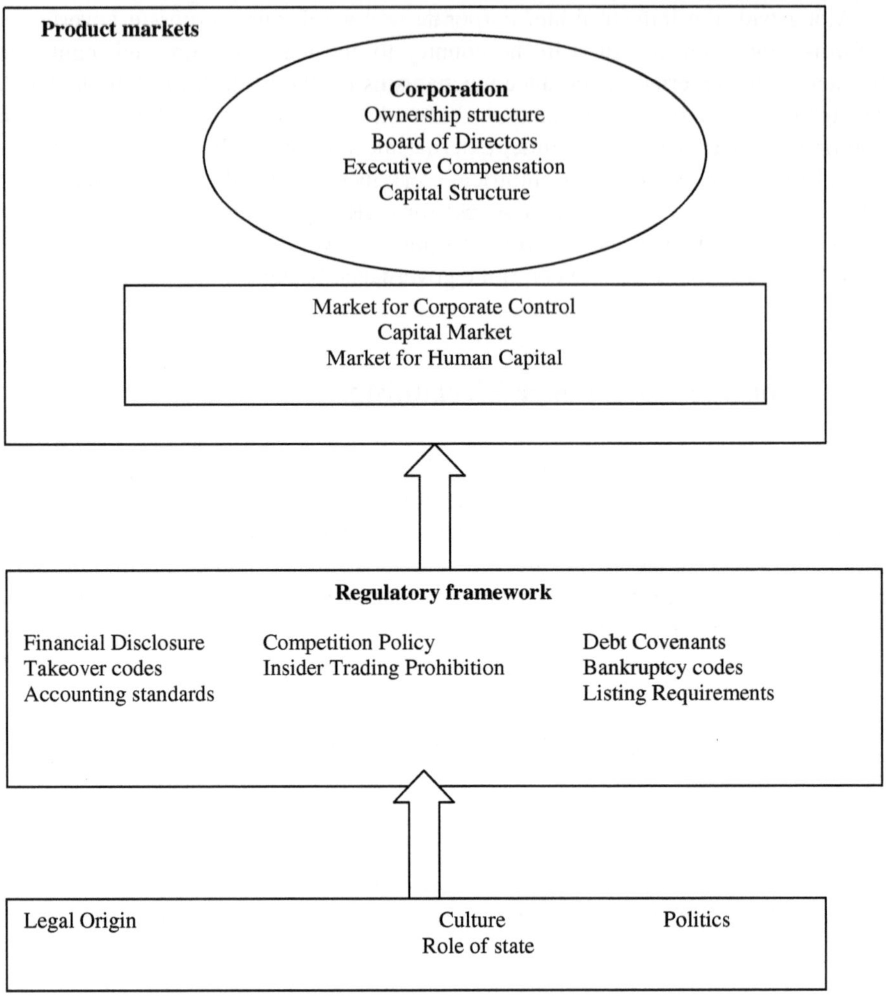

Fig. 5.1 Corporate Governance: big picture

control, and on the other hand, due to their substantial control over corporate decisions, they can pursue private benefits. This issue is more important when controlling owners are wealthy families or other firms that, themselves are controlled by wealthy families. This is a common feature of most of the other developed and developing and emerging countries. As with large shareholders in US and UK, family ownership has some advantages like: (1) being free of manager-owner agency problem, (2) because of family values, they are better able to manage corporate affairs smoothly. On the other hand, there is also an evidence of another type of agency problem which is appropriation of resources through tunneling

(Bertrand et al. 2002). The new generation of research modifies agency problem as conflicts of interest between large shareholders and small investors. Several studies on Continental Europe and Asia have followed since then.[5]

B. **Capital Structure**

This mechanism deals with the choice of debt to solve the governance problem. It is argued in the literature that debt has more disciplining power than the equity as it limits the extent of inefficiency of the management, if the management wants to repay the debt. The banks can monitor corporate based on short term lending procedures in that if the management does not seem to be able to repay its debt the bank can stop further lending to the company. Moreover, debt may force the management to give up control in case it cannot make a predetermined repayment to the claimholders. The agency aspect of capital structure summarizes debt as more powerful instrument in constraining the management and protecting the outside investor than the ordinary equity based incentive scheme.

C. **Board of Directors**

1. The board consists of a collective group of individuals elected by the shareholders of a corporation to oversee the management of the corporation. Functions of a board are: (1) to provide strategic guidance of the management, and (2) effectively monitor the decisions pursued by the management. The primary issue is board's accountability to the company and shareholders. These issues are further related to the proportion of executive directors, who are also the members of the management and the non-executive directors who may be the representatives of the company's major purchasers, suppliers or the chief executives of the other firm. The key issue is the independence of the board to ensure the balance of power and accountability of the system. The related issue is to sustain the independence when the CEO and chairman are the same person (Duality) which in turn reflects concentration of control in the hands of CEO. Empirical literature indicates significant differences in firm performance with firms opting for independent leadership consistently outperformed those relying upon CEO duality (for example see Rechner and Dalton 2006).

D. **Executive Compensation**

This issue is important because it directly provides enough incentives to top executives to align their incentives with those of shareholders. The primary issues are sensitivity of pay to performance of these executives to ensure that their efforts are directly related to company's performance.

[5]See Claessens et al. (2000) for East-Asian firms, Faccio and Lang (2002) for Western Europe, Dennis and McConnell (2003) on survey of international corporate governance, and the papers cited in there.

5.2.2 External Corporate Governance Mechanisms

E. **Legal and Regulatory framework**

Shleifer and Vishny (1997) emphasize that the differences in legal origins and the effectiveness in enforcing the laws across countries is the better way to understand corporate governance. LaPorta et al. (1998) find out that the quality of legal protection is best in Common law countries and the French and German Civil law countries are worse in protecting minority investors. Stulz et al. (2004) find that at a given level of investor protection in a country, better corporate governance mechanisms are more likely to be accepted at the firm level as country's financial and economic development improves.

F. **Market for Corporate Control**

If other company believes that it can improve the performance of the firm either by altering the composition of the management will offer either a friendly tender to buy the equities held by public or if the incumbent management is not supporting this transaction, will make a hostile takeover bid (see Grossman and Hart 1980 for a comprehensive literature on takeovers). On one hand, takeovers and mergers act ac disciplining mechanisms, takeovers can lead to increase in agency costs by allowing managers to expand their empire or overpaying by the bidding management that will bring them private benefits of control. Besides, takeovers require a liquid capital market so that bidders can raise capital on short notice. Therefore, in the countries with less liquid markets this mechanism might not work as an effective control mechanism.

There is another body of literature that goes beyond the country level to explain variation in governance mechanisms across countries by including characteristics like legal origin, culture, economic and political factors (see LaPorta et al. 2000; Rajan and Zingales 2003; Roe 2003). All the firms operate in their respective product markets and irrespective of different types of agency problems, each firm is subject to the product market competition, which in itself acts as an ultimate discipline.

Finally, stylized theories of product market competition imply that corporate governance will be automatically taken into care when the product markets are competitive since if the company fails to maximize the profits then the company will have to exit the market. Kaplan (1999) argues that the corporate governance is needed when the company is matured or operating in a non competitive industry since then there will be resources to waste and no compulsion to maximize for survival. When the management can waste substantial amount of resources then the need for minority investor protection should be taken care of. The usual argument is that in the longer run, the corporate governance system evolved will be optimal but the time lag is very long.

5.3 Corporate Governance in India

With 20 million shareholders India is one of the largest emerging markets. The concern of corporate governance in India was coupled with industrial reforms in 1991. Trade and other structural reforms in the country are manifestations of desire of policymakers to put efficient allocation and use of resources at the heart of economic activity. Among other things, this depends upon whether a firm's management can be induced to use resources efficiently and this is why corporate governance as an issue becomes important. Majority of large corporations are controlled by wealthy families and business houses. Family control through pyramids[6] and cross shareholdings further separates control from cash flow rights. Controlling owners hold control over the management through persons acting in concert which are usually private companies controlled by promoters. In such a way a divergence between ownership and control is present in most of the family controlled companies. This divergence generates incentives for expropriation of minority shareholders' wealth. Therefore, the issue of corporate governance in India is primarily that of regulating the controlling shareholder and protecting the rights of small investors. Having realized this, ongoing corporate sector reforms are aimed towards encouraging the participation by other equity holders' like domestic and foreign institutional investors and increasing the awareness of small investors. Development financial institutions (DFI) play an important role as a provider of long-term finance and commercial banks play an important role as a provider of short-term working capital. Since liberalization foreign investors and private corporate bodies have emerged as large-block shareholders.[7]

Initiative of good corporate governance came from the industrial association of India—the Confederation of Indian Industry (CII) which drafted the country's first Code for Desirable Corporate Governance in 1998. Large corporations of India responded positively and adopted the recommendations of the CII code. Later in 2000, India's capital market regulator, Securities of Exchange Board of India (SEBI) formulated the country's first code of best practices in corporate governance. The CII and SEBI codes have emphasized the independence of board, specified the structure of audit and remuneration committees, and outlined the accounting standards for financial reporting. The recommendations of the code were instituted through a new Clause 49 in the listing agreement. Positive effect of passage of the Clause reflected in stock market gains for large and medium sized firms (Black and Khanna 2007). Since 1997, SEBI has modified the existing takeover code to facilitate an efficient market for corporate control.

[6]According to LaPorta et al. (1999), a firm's ownership structure is a pyramid if it has an ultimate owner and there is at least one publicly traded company between it and the ultimate owner.

[7]Sarkar and Sarkar (2000) provide an informative study on India's financial and banking sector development. Goswami (2002), Chakrabarti et al. (2008) presents the state of corporate governance pre- and post-reforms.

Since 2000 there has been a series of revisions introduced in Clause 49 to incorporate the recommendations of committees such as Naresh Chandra Committee (2002) and Narayan Murthy Committee (2003). Following the corporate scandals of the US, the Department of Corporate Affairs (DCA), government of India set up the Naresh Chandra Committee to examine corporate governance issues focusing on role of auditors and audit committee. Many recommendations of the report are incorporated in the Companies Act 2013. Later, Narayan Murthy committee was constituted by SEBI to review the performance of corporate governance in the country as well as to determine the role of companies in responding to rumour and other price sensitive information circulating in the market in order to enhance the transparency and integrity of the market (SEBI 2003). Based on the recommendations of these committees and public comments received, amendments were made in Clause 49 of the Listing Agreement and revised Clause 49 came into effect since 2005 which formulates the corporate governance in new and existing companies listed on the stock exchanges of India. The Clause 49 revises the requirements of board structure and conduct significantly by defining independent director and board independence explicitly for the first time since the reforms. In addition, recommendations about the code of conduct and formation of audit committee were mandated through this Clause.

Concentration of ownership in the hands of families is a dominant feature of several countries including India. Family control through pyramids and cross shareholdings generates a different sort of agency problem that is not generally the case in widely held firms. This is the intercorporate transfer of resources among pyramid firms to advantage the controlling shareholder. This phenomenon is called Tunneling (Johnson et al. 2000). Family firms are dominant all over the world. The distinguishing features of family firms are presence of controlling owners who are usually the family members who either run the corporation themselves or hire professional managers. Due to their large shareholdings and control managers in these family firms serve their interest. On one hand, controlling ownership in these firms have positive firm value driven by family reputation and wealth effects associated with large shareholdings, on the other hand, they have the power to pursue their private benefits. This conflict of interest worsens in countries with poor legal and regulatory environment. There is another distinguishing feature of family firm through which they maintain a separation of ownership and control- through pyramiding or cross shareholding. This separation of cash flow rights and control rights have negative impact on most of the companies in Europe and Asia (Faccio and Lang 2002; Claessens et al. 2000). In India controlling owners are wealthy families who use control pyramids and cross shareholdings to exert control over the management. On an average the wedge between promoters' direct ownership (cash flow rights) and total control (through Persons Acting in Concert) is 10 %. The other large investors are institutional investors and other corporate bodies. Since 2001, DFIs have become more market oriented and hence one could expect more monitoring incentives for these institutions. It would be an interesting question to explore how non-controlling owners affect firm value especially when they hold substantial voting rights to alter management decision. There is also an argument that large institutional investors do not co-ordinate even if they form a block together (Black and coffee 1994). Selarka (2005) explores this issue of coordination between top two outsiders in Indian companies and finally if the effect depends on whether these outside shareholders are institutional investors, financial institutions, foreign investors or other corporations. She includes a wider set of mechanisms, such as identity and ownership of outside block shareholders holding at least 5 % of total equity of the firm. The study provides a closer look at the role of institutional investors to see if these investors align their interests to constrain the insiders from expropriating corporate resources especially when these investors hold significant voting rights. Based on analysis of 1397 listed firms, she finds a U shaped relationship between controlling owners' shareholding and firm performance with a turning point at approximately 47 %. This is significantly higher than 26 % reported by Sarkar and Sarkar (2000) which can be corroborated to the detailed ownership data post 2000 which was available to Selarka (2005). More recently, using a pooled data between 2001 and 2004, Pant and Pattanayak (2007) find two turning points, similar to Morck et al. (1988), with firm value increasing at low level (0–29 %) and very high levels (56 % and above) of insider stakes and negative at the intermediate levels. These studies demonstrate the benefits of concentrated ownership over expropriation effects associated with high insider stakes.[8]

Along with several recommendations on internal corporate governance mechanisms India has modified its takeover act in 1997 to facilitate exit mechanisms for small investors as well as to increase power of minority outside investors. Role of minority investor is recognized through a mandatory bid if any investor's shares other than the controlling owner exceed 15 % of the total equity. In principle, if managers are entrenched and waste resources, firm's actual value will be much less than potential value. This would attract other management teams to compete for the firm and finally an acquiring firm will replace the incumbent management. Therefore, takeovers and mergers act as external mechanisms. However, in addition to being a potential solution to the manager/shareholder agency problem, takeover market can be a manifestation of manager/shareholder agency problem. Mangers can waste resources by overpaying for acquisitions rather than returning cash to the shareholders. The literature is divided in its opinion about the impact of concentration of ownership on firm performance. On the one hand, concentration of ownership that, in turn, concentrates management control in the hands of a strategic investor eliminates agency problems associated with dispersed ownership. On the other hand, it opens up the possibility of conflict of interest between the entrenched strategic investor and other stakeholders of the firms like the smaller shareholders. Bhaumik and Selarka (2012) examine the impact of mergers, takeover and acquisitions on firm performance and draws conclusions about the impact of concentrated ownership and entrenchment of owner-managers in an emerging market context.

[8]For more details on concentrated ownership and firm performance see Chap. 4 in Sarkar and Sarkar (2012).

Finally, there is a stylized theory that product market competition as an ultimate solution is that regardless of separation of ownership and control (Berle and Means 1932), competitive selection process in the product markets would ensure that managers are obliged to maximize profits (Alchain 1950; Friedman 1953; Stigler 1958). On the other hand, competition alone may not solve a problem of corporate governance because product market competition may reduce the returns on capital and hence cut the amount that managers can possibly expropriate, but it does not prevent managers from expropriating the competitive return after the capital is sunk (Shliefer and Vishny 1997). Moreover, insufficient role of product market competition is explained in terms of imperfect competition, which need not pose the exit threat on entrenched managers in the short run. Therefore, competition alone might be insufficient and role of corporate governance in a firm is to ensure that the signals and other relevant information are actually translated into investment decisions (Berglof and Thaddan 1999). In fact, corporate governance and product market competition together are needed to be corrected because capital markets constrain managers weakly when product market competition is weak (Roe 2003). Therefore, theory poses an empirical question of interaction between corporate governance and product market competition—the two can act as substitutes or complements. This is an interesting research issue for India where dominance of family and business group ownership might take longer for corporate governance mechanisms to change. Selarka (2014) explores this interaction between product market competition and corporate governance by arguing that corporate governance is a multifaceted measure. She explores the role of corporate governance by creating an encompassing index of corporate governance based on several elements of internal governance such as board of directors, ownership structure, audit quality and disclosure of information.

5.4 Conclusion

Most of the existing studies on corporate governance based on agency theory have examined its impact on firm performance and strategic decisions such as mergers and acquisitions (M&As), capital structure, dividend payout etc. As the concept of corporate governance is embedded into the process of resource allocation which ultimately affects the organisational behaviour in general, under the shareholder value maximisation paradigm it is often argued that corporate governance will have an impact on the decision of CSR spending as it is a management decision of resource allocation after the shareholder value is being realized (Aras and Crowther 2007; Friedman 1970; Jones et al. 1997). Therefore, following Freidman (1970) we propose a framework to develop an empirical model to analyze the effect of corporate governance on CSR. This framework incorporates the agency problem between management and non-controlling shareholders which may arise as CSR spending is primarily allocated out of shareholders value. This interaction between corporate governance and CSR is well suited in the Indian setting as the recent Companies Act 2013 mandates allocating 2 % of the profit as CSR expenditure. Our study focuses on large Indian firms between 2010 and 2012 prior to the Companies Act 2013 and hence presents a unique opportunity for a natural experiment to analyze the interaction between quality of governance and its effect of CSR activities undertaken by firms in India in an unconstrained environment.

References

Alchain AA (1950) Uncertainty, evolution and economic theory. J Polit Econ 58(6):211–221

Aras G, Crowther D (2007) What level of trust is needed for sustainability? Soc Responsib J 3(3):60–68

Berglof E, von Thadden EL (1999) The changing corporate governance paradigm: implications for transition and developing countries. William davidson institute working papers series 263, William davidson institute at the university of michigan

Berle A, Means G (1932) The modern corporation and private property, MacMillan, New York

Bertrand M, Mehta P, Mullainathan S (2002) Ferreting out tunneling: an application to indian business groups. Q J Econ 2002 117(1):121–148

Bhaumik S, Selarka E (2012) Does ownership concentration improve M&A outcomes in emerging markets?: evidence from India. J corp financ 18(4):717–726

Black B, Coffee J (1994) Hail britannia?: institutional investor behavior under limited regulation. Michigan law review, pp 1997–2087

Black BS, Khanna VS (2007) Can corporate governance reforms increase firm market values? event study evidence from india. J Empirical Legal Stud 4:749–796

Blair M (1995) Ownership and control: rethinking corporate governance for the twenty-first century, Brookings Institution, Washington DC

Cadbury A (1992) The committee on the financial aspects of corporate governance, Gee and Company, London

Chakrabarti R, Megginson W, Yadav PK (2008) Corporate governance in India. J Appl Corp Financ 20(1):59–72

Claessens S (2006) Corporate Governance and Development. World Bank Res Obser 21(1):91–122

Claessens S, Fan JPH (2002) Corporate Governance in Asia: A Survey. Int Rev Financ 3:71–103

Claessens S, Djankov S, Lang LHP (2000) The separation of ownership and control in east asian corporations. J Financ Econ 58:81–112

Committee on the financial aspects of corporate governance (1992) Report of the committee on the financial aspects of corporate governance (Cadbury Report). Gee, London

Core J, Guay W, Larcker D (2003) Executive equity compensation and incentives: a survey. Econ Policy Rev 9(1):27–50

Demsetz H, Lehn K (1985) The structure of corporate ownership: causes and consequences. J Polit Econ 1155–1177

Denis DK, McConnell JJ (2003) International corporate governance. J financ quant anal 38(01):1–36

Faccio M, Lang L (2002) The ultimate ownership of western european companies. J Financ Econ 65:365–395

Friedman M (1953) The methodology of positive economics. in essays in positive economics, University of Chicago Press, Chicago

Friedman M (1970) The social responsibility of business is to increase profits. NY Times Mag 32–33:122—126

Goswami O (2002) Corporate governance in india. In: taking action against corruption in asia and the pacific (Manila: Asian Development Bank)

Harris M, Raviv A (1988) Corporate governance: voting rights and majority rules. J Financ Econ 20:175–202

Hermalin BE, Weisbach MS (2002) Boards of directors as an endogenously determined institution: a survey of the economic literature. Economic policy review

Holderness CG (2002) A survey of blockholders and corporate control. Economic Policy Review. pp 51–64

Holmstrom B, Kaplan SN (2001) Corporate governance and merger activity in the us: making sense of the 1980's and 1990's. Working Paper, NBER

Jensen M, Meckling W (1976) Theory of the firm: managerial behavior, agency costs, and ownership structure. J Financ Econ 3:305–360

John K, Senbet LW (1998) Corporate governance and board effectiveness. J Bank Financ 22:371–403

Johnson S, La Porta R, Lopez-Silanes F, Shleifer A (2000) Tunneling. Am Econ Rev 90:22–27

Jones C, Hesterly WS, Borgatti SP (1997) A general theory of network governance: exchange conditions and social mechanisms. Acad Manag J 22(4):911–945

Kaplan SN (1999) Top executive incentives in Germany, Japan and the USA: a comparison. In: Carpenter J, Yermack D (eds) Executive compensation and shareholder value theory and evidence

Karpoff J (1998) Impact of shareholder activism on target companies: a survey of empirical findings. Unpublished paper, University of Washington

LaPorta R, Lopez-de-Silanes F, Shleifer A, Vishny R (1997) Legal determinants of external finance. J Financ 52(3):1131–1150

LaPorta R, Lopez-de-Silanes F, Shleifer A (1998) Law and finance. J Polit Econ106(6)

LaPorta R, Lopez-de-Silanes F, Shleifer A (1999) Corporate Ownership around the World. J Financ 54(2):471–517

LaPorta R, Lopez-de-Silanes F, Shleifer A, Vishny R (2000) Investor protection and corporate governance. J Financ Econ 58(1):3−27

Morck R, Shleifer A, Vishny RW (1988) Managerial ownership and market valuation: An empirical analysis. J Financ Econ 20:292–315

Murphy K (1999) Executive Compensation. In: Ashenfelter O, Card D (eds) Handbook of Labor Economics, (Vol. 3). Amsterdam, North Holland

Pant M, Pattanayak M (2007) Insider ownership and firm value: evidence from Indian corporate sector. Economic and Political Weekly. Accessed 21 April 2007

Rajan RG, Zingales L (2003) The great reversals: the politics of financial development in the 20th century. J Financ Econ 69(1):5–50

Rechner PL, Dalton DR (2006) CEO duality and organizational performance: a longitudinal analysis. Strat Mgmt J 12:155–160

Roe MJ (2003) Political determinants of corporate governance. Oxford university press

Sarkar J, Sarkar S (2000) Large shareholder activism in corporate governance in developing countries: evidence from india. Int Rev Financ 1(3):161–194

Sarkar J, Sarkar S (2012) Corporate governance in india. Sage publications, New Delhi

SEBI Committee on Corporate Governance (2003): A report

Selarka E (2005) Ownership Concentration and Firm Value: A Study from the Indian Corporate Sector. Emerg Mark Financ Tr 41(6):83–108

Selarka E (2014) Corporate governance, product market competition and firm performance: evidence from india. In: Boubaker S, Khuong Nguyen D (eds) Corporate governance in emerging markets. pp 55–77

Shleifer A, Vishny RW (1986) Large shareholders and corporate control. J Polit Econ 461–488

Shleifer A, Vishny RW (1997) A Survey of Corporate Governance. J Financ LII(2):737–783

Smith A (1776) Wealth of Nations. The modern library, New York

Stigler GJ (1958) The Economics of Scale. J Law Econ 1:54–71

Stulz R, Karolyi GA, Doidge C (2004) Why do countries matter so much for corporate governance? ECGI Finance Working Paper No 50/2004

Tirole J (2001) Corporate Governance. Econometrica 69:1–35

Chapter 6
CSR Activities in Large Indian Firms—Descriptive Statistics

6.1 Introduction

Indian companies started disclosing their nonfinancial statements which includes information on CSR and related activities only very recently which makes it a difficult assignment to capture the actual CSR spending. In this chapter we investigate the information structure of CSR related activities and expenditure by drawing patterns across disclosure of initiatives and disclosure of expenditures. We go through all possible sources of information such as annual reports, websites, business responsibility reports etc. to gather understanding about each company's activities that can be related to social responsibility in a broader sense. We observe that Indian companies disclose CSR expenditure under various heads and terms, and not necessarily as "CSR Expenditure" as one category. During the data collection exercise, we find that companies disclose CSR spending information under different heads like donations, charity, CSR Budget, Allocation, Reserves, Provisions, Social Welfare expenses in "other expenditure".

As highlighted in the previous section a few studies employ quantified information on social responsibility in terms of disclosure and execution. Given this backdrop we address this limitation by making an attempt to study the status of CSR reporting practices and accounting for the actual CSR spending of largest 500 Indian companies.

6.2 Sample Selection

We design data collection based on the functional concept of CSR in India. As per the Companies Act, 2013 it is the large firms which are obligated to undertake CSR activities and to disclosure the relevant information. Therefore, we select the largest 500 Indian companies which are listed on the Bombay Stock Exchange (BSE) based on market capitalisation in financial year 2012. Our sample covers nearly 70 % of the total market capitalisation of BSE in 2012. The selection of the

S.N. Bhaduri and E. Selarka, *Corporate Governance and Corporate Social Responsibility of Indian Companies*, CSR, Sustainability, Ethics & Governance,
DOI 10.1007/978-981-10-0925-9_6

period of study is also of importance as 2009–10 to 2011–12 which is just prior to year the Companies Act 2013 is implemented. This provides us an opportunity to understand the status and preparedness of Indian firms in the context of CSR. We also gather information on financial indicators such as size, age, and leverage along with shareholding pattern from Prowess.[1] After excluding missing observations we obtain 1497 firm-year observations.

As there is no uniformity or standard format available for the CSR reporting, we capture the CSR spending by collecting all the relevant available information on the amount spent for social responsibilities with a cautious effort of avoiding double counting. We generate CSR spending variables based on the actual expenditure as well as disclosure of activities across categories listed in Table 6.1. Table 6.1 also presents the detailed list of variables and their description. As variables capturing the disclosure of CSR activities are descriptive in nature, we code each disclosure based variable as a dummy variable that equals 1 if they disclose relevant information and 0 otherwise. These categories are drawn from seven categories based on the provisions of the recent Companies Act 2013 Schedule VII (Table 6.2). The CSR expenditure and disclosure information are had collected from Annual Reports, Corporate Sustainability Report, Business Responsibility Report and the company's website. Further CSR Identity database is also used to validate the social activities for the sample during 2009–10 to 2011–12.

6.3 Reporting Statistics on CSR Expenditure

Preliminary analysis shows that the number of companies disclosing their CSR activities increased from 61 to 76 % over the sample period (2010–2012). Large Indian firms have started disclosing their social responsibility activities in recent years with a gradual increase of about 15 % in last three years since the draft Companies Bill was proposed in 2009.

In terms of the social initiatives the majority of the companies reported community development initiatives like agriculture, eradicating poverty, empowerment of women, livelihood, unemployment and rural development which further increased from 49 to 61 % during the sample years followed by education where the percentage of reporting companies increased from 45 to 59 %. Healthcare is another sector which has witnessed a significant increase with the percentage of companies reporting from 13 to 18 % during the period of study.

Figure 6.1 presents the distribution of sample companies disclosing information about CSR activities under the seven categories during 2010–2012. The overall picture reveals that, Community development, Education and Health care are the major sectors where companies focus on social activities. More recently the new areas of CSR activities such as Sports, Disaster relief, Arts and Culture as part of

[1]Prowess is a database compiled by Centre for Monitoring India Economy (CMIE) and is widely used for analysis of audited financial information.

Table 6.1 Description of parameters to compile CSR by Indian companies

Parameters	Description
Panel A: CSR expenditure (Rs. crore)	
Donations	Spending reported under expense in the financial statement as Donations
Political donation	Spending reported under expense in the financial statement as donations made to political parties
Charity	Spending reported under expense in the financial statement as charitable contributions/charity
Donation and charity	Spending reported under expense in the financial statement as Donation and Charity
CSR spending	CSR Spending disclosure in the Annual Report/Sustainability Development Report/Business Responsibility Report under CSR Section. Generally reported as CSR Spending, Community Investment, Voluntary donations and like
CSR expenditure	Spending reported under expense in the financial statement as CSR Activities
CSR allocation	Reported as Allocation/Budget for CSR. We check with the previous year unspent CSR amount to confirm this entry
CSR reserves	CSR reserves. We check with the previous year unspent CSR amount to confirm this entry
CSR provisions	Provisions for CSR. We check with the previous year unspent CSR amount to confirm this entry
Education expenditure	Expenditure on Education. Includes expenses reported in terms of scholarships for the marginalized sections, Children education, Vocational Training, Skill building trainings and workshops for both employees and needy society
Health care expenditure	Expenditure on Health care. Includes expenses reported on health care, child health, elderly care, women health, disabled assistance, medical camps, HIV/AIDS awareness programs, Pulse Polio, eye, Blood Donation, ambulances to Medical centres/Hospitals/NGOs, hearing aids/wheel chairs to physically challenged, financial assistance/medical equipment to hospitals, health schemes for employees etc.
Disaster relief expenditure	Expenditure on Disaster Relief. Includes expenses reported on national and local disaster reliefs like floods, earthquake, cyclones etc.
Environmental expenditure	Expenditure on Environmental protection. Includes expenses on environmental and energy management, climate change, Rain Water Harvesting, Water Management, carbon emission control, waste generation, Forests protection etc.
Community development expenditure	Expenditure on Community Development. Includes expenses on providing drinking water, constructing infrastructure, village development and adoption, agriculture, eradicating poverty, empowerment of women, livelihood, Accidents and Road Safety, Animal Welfare, Unemployment etc.
Sports expenditure	Expenditure on Sports Development. Includes expenses on conducting/sponsoring sports events

(continued)

Table 6.1 (continued)

Parameters	Description
Heritage expenditure	Expenditure on preserving/renovating national heritage. Includes expenses on building temples, culture, music, dance or art exhibition
Panel B: CSR disclosure	
Educational disclosure	Equals 1 if company reports activities undertaken specific to education such as supporting primary education, sponsorships etc.; 0 otherwise
Educational beneficiaries	Number of people/villages/districts benefited from company's educational program
Healthcare disclosure	Equals 1 if company reports activities undertaken specific to health such as people covered, beds to hospitals, healthcare, childcare etc.; 0 otherwise
Health care beneficiaries	Number of people/villages/districts benefited from company's health program
Community disclosure	Equals 1 if company reports activities undertaken specific to community development such as people covered under constructing infrastructure, village development and adoption, agriculture, eradicating poverty, empowerment of women, livelihood unemployment, rural development; 0 otherwise
Community beneficiaries	Number of people/villages/districts benefited from company's community development program
Environmental disclosure	Equals 1 if company reports activities undertaken specific to environment protection and energy management; 0 otherwise
Sports disclosure	Equals 1 if company reports activities undertaken specific to sports such as sponsoring sports events or and promoting a particular sport; 0 otherwise
Disaster relief disclosure	Equals 1 if company reports activities undertaken specific to disaster relief such as donations made/set up camps for natural calamities, flood, draught, earthquake, Tsunami etc.; 0 otherwise
Heritage disclosure	Equals 1 if company reports activities undertaken specific to Art and Heritage such as sponsored activities on heritage, culture and like; 0 otherwise
Location	Area of focus for implementing aforementioned CSR activities. Includes location or area of implementing the social responsibility programmes or activities

social initiatives have also gained prominence. The overall trend shows an increase in reporting initiatives as well as the scope of areas covered under social activities over the sample period.

Proportion of companies spending on community development is highest among different categories of CSR contributions across sample companies followed by education and health related activities. Among other categories, environmental protection, sports and preservation of heritage are emerging as sources of CSR activities by sample companies.

Table 6.2 Description of categories to allocate CSR spending by Indian companies

Parameter category of CSR	Description
Education	Includes information disclosed regarding educational activities such as scholarships for the Marginalized sections, Children education, Primary, secondary, Higher Secondary and College Education, Vocational Training, Skill building trainings and workshops for needy society, and Building Schools, Educational Institutions, Colleges and training centres in India. Under this category we also record the number of persons benefited under the aforementioned CSR activities related to Education
Health care	Includes information disclosed regarding Health care, Child Health, Elderly/Old age Care, Women Health, Disabled Assistance, medical camps, HIV/AIDS awareness, Pulse Polio, Eye, Blood Donation, ambulances to Medical centres/ Hospitals/NGOs, hearing aids/wheel chairs to physically challenged, financial assistance/medical equipment to hospitals, Health schemes for employees etc Under this category we also record the number of persons benefited under the aforementioned CSR activities related to Health care
Community	Includes information disclosed regarding drinking water, constructing infrastructure, village development and adoption, agriculture, eradicating poverty, Empowerment of women, livelihood, Accidents and Road Safety, Animal Welfare, Unemployment, Rural Development. Under this category we also record the number of persons benefited under the aforementioned CSR activities related to Community development
Environment	Includes information disclosed regarding Environmental and energy management, climate change, Rain Water harvesting, Water Management, carbon emission control, waste generation, Forests protection, Environmental protection
Sport	Includes information disclosed such as conducting and encouraging sports events, sponsoring development related to sports
Disaster relief	Includes information disclosed regarding donations for national and local disaster reliefs like floods, earthquake, cyclones, tsunami, etc.
Heritage, art and culture	Includes information disclosed such as spending on building temples, culture, music and dance, art Exhibition, preserving/ renovating national heritage

We also capture the total amount spent on social activities by sample companies in each year of study. Figure 6.2 presents the distribution of total CSR expenditure across these activities which are categorised according to Schedule VII. Education related activities significantly dominate the CSR expenditure in the sample for each period followed by community development, healthcare and environment protection related contributions.

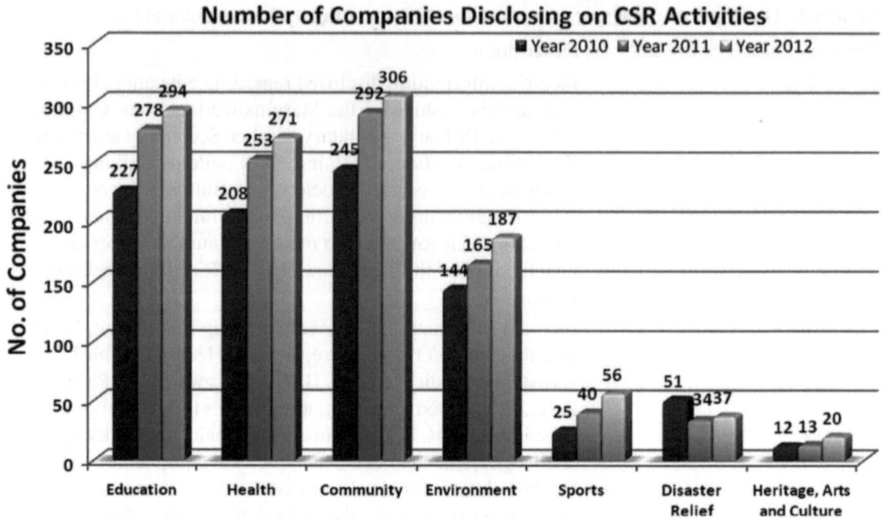

Fig. 6.1 Number of companies disclosing CSR activities (2010–2012). *Source* Authors' compilation based on the hand collected data on large 500 companies between 2010 and 2012

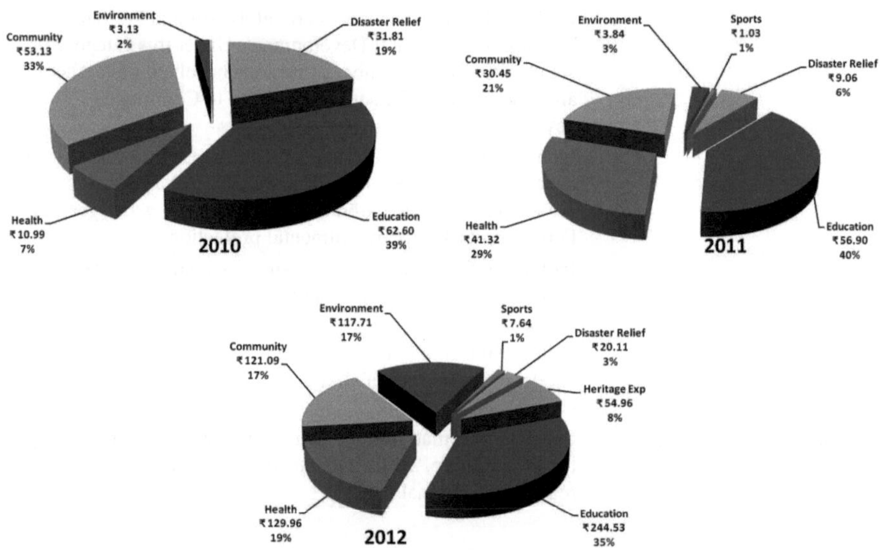

Fig. 6.2 Sector-wise CSR Spending. *Notes* Amounts are Rs. crore. Compiled from Authors' compilation based on the hand collected data on large 500 companies during 2010–2012

A significant change has taken place as healthcare contributions witnessed a significant increase from 7 to 29 % between 2010 and 2011. During the study period from 2010 to 2012 the contributions to natural disasters like flood, cyclone, storm, drought, and tsunami reduced from 19 % to 3 %. Also contributions to environment protection related activities significantly increased from 3 % in 2010 to 17 % in 2012 followed by the draft Companies Bill. Similarly, new areas such as Sports, Heritage, Arts and Cultural development acquire about 9 % of the total CSR contributions during the year 2011–12 followed by the Companies Bill in 2011. Such an increase in new categories is compensated by the marginal reduction in other two major categories viz community development and healthcare respectively.

6.4 Patterns in CSR Expenditure Across Activities

This section describes the pattern in CSR expenditure of our sample firms drawn from their standalone and consolidated annual statements. We conduct this exercise to understand the patterns in CSR contributions at the standalone company level as well as consolidated through its group companies. Figure 6.3 presents the actual amount spent on activities in standalone and consolidated statements. In addition, donations which are the primary source of CSR prior to the Companies Bill in 2011 has witnessed significant reduction. This further translated into increase in explicit reporting of CSR allocation and CSR reserves in the standalone balance sheets since 2011. This indicates that companies responded to the recommendation of Companies Bill positively and in a more explicit manner. One of the differences in standalone and consolidated balance sheets is that consolidated balance sheets report higher actual expenses whereas standalone balance sheets report higher allocated or reserved funds for CSR. Also, political donations reported in both standalone as well as consolidated annual statements decline significantly over the sample period.

6.5 Univariate Analysis of Top and Bottom Ten Companies

This section presents the status of our sample companies with respect to the 2 % PAT rule specified in the Companies Act 2013. Table 6.3 presents distribution of companies that report CSR expenditure more than or equal to 2 % of preceding three years average PAT during sample period. The proportion of companies increased from 20 % to 22 % between 2010 and 2011 followed by decline to 19 % in 2012. The second column indicates the average CSR expenditure as a proportion of preceding three years average PAT for sample companies during each sample period. The average CSR spending as a proportion of last three years average PAT increased from 1.39 to 2.03 % in 2012 which indicates that large companies responded positively to the recommendation of Companies Bill by increasing allocation and spending on social activities in 2012 which is just prior to the Companies Act 2013.

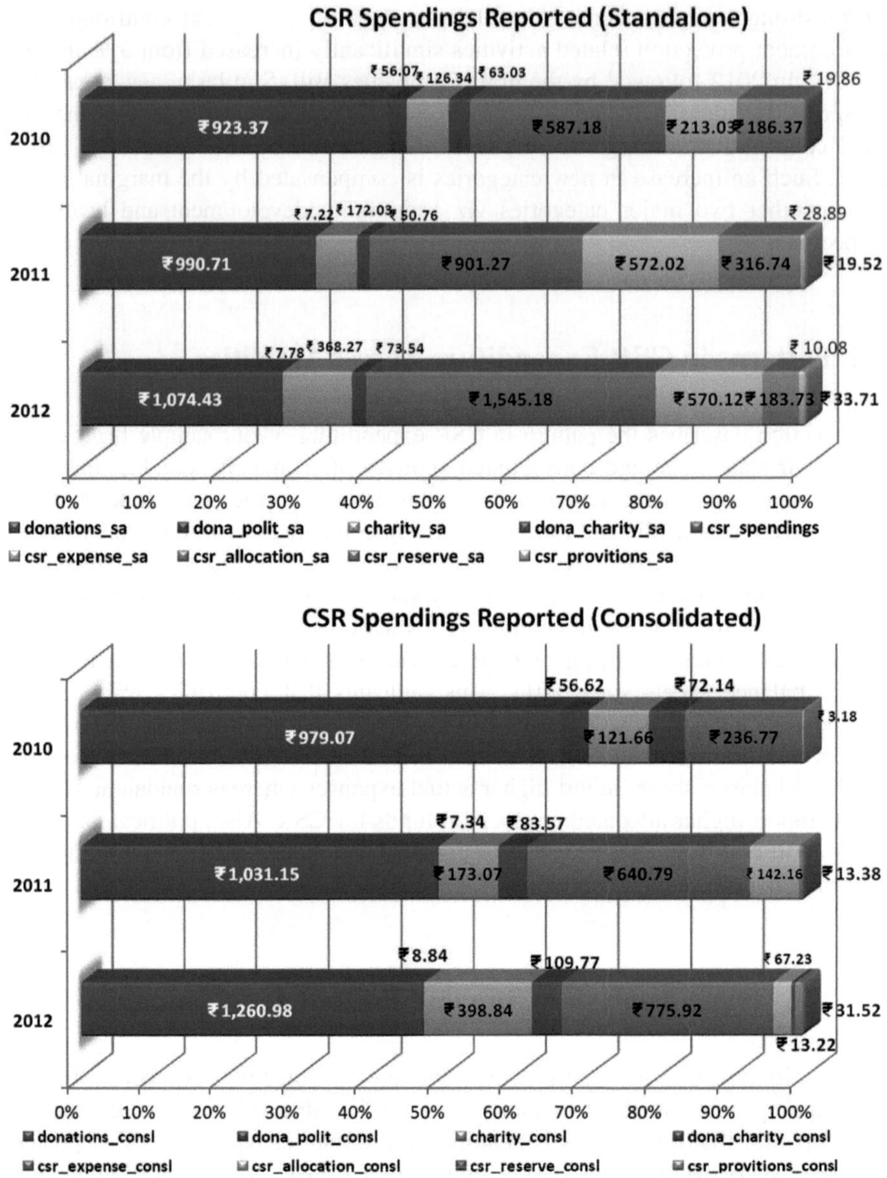

Fig. 6.3 CSR spending in standalone and consolidated accounts of large 500 companies (2011–2013)

Further, in subsequent subsections we report the firm characteristics to highlight whether their exists structural differences between the top and bottom ten companies ranked as per two criterion: (1) based on actual spending on CSR and (2) based on CSR expenditure as a percentage of the three years average PAT.

Table 6.3 Companies contribution towards CSR spending as percentage of PAT

Year	Number of companies CSR spending more than or equal to 2 % of last three years average PAT (% of companies)	Average CSR spending as a percentage of last three years PAT
2009–10	101 (20.24 %)	1.39
2010–11	113 (22.64 %)	1.77
2011–12	95 (19.03 %)	2.03

Source Authors' calculation based on the hand collected data on CSR expenditure and disclosure for large 500 companies listed on BSE during 2010–12

6.5.1 Ownership Structure and CSR Spending

In this section, we describe the ownership structure and shareholding pattern of the top and bottom ten companies ranked as per the two criterion described earlier across each year in the study period. Table 6.4 reports the number of companies classified into four ownership structures viz central government, business group affiliates, foreign or multinationals, and Indian standalone. The table shows that Central Government owned companies and large business groups outperform standalone and foreign owned companies on actual CSR spending. However, this is not consistent with the percentage of PAT spent by these companies where business group affiliates and standalone companies dominate the central government companies.

In the bottom ranking there is a decline from 60 to 20 % in number of group companies and a rise from 20 to 50 % in the number of MNCs and Private Indian companies. Further Table 6.5 reports the shareholding pattern of Top and Bottom ten companies. The shareholding pattern is drawn from reporting under the Clause 35 where every listed company is required to report shareholdings of promoters and non-promoters. Promoters are further reported as Indian promoters and foreign promoters. Non-promoter institutions is the second largest category among

Table 6.4 Number of top and bottom ten companies across ownership structures

Based on actual CSR spending	2010		2011		2012	
	Top	Bottom	Top	Bottom	Top	Bottom
Central government	5	0	7	1	4	0
Indian business groups	4	1	2	1	4	2
MNCs/foreign	0	3	0	3	1	2
Indian standalone	1	6	1	5	1	6
Based on percentage of PAT spent						
Central government	0	1	2	2	2	0
Indian business groups	1	1	3	2	3	2
MNCs/foreign	1	3	1	1	2	2
Indian standalone	8	5	4	5	3	6

Table 6.5 Ownership structure (% of total shares) of Top and Bottom Ten Companies based on actual CSR spending and percentage of PAT

Based on actual CSR spending	2010		2011		2012	
	Top	Bottom	Top	Bottom	Top	Bottom
Promoters	57	65	57	53	53	49
	(−0.977)		(0.231)		(0.331)	
Indian promoters	52	44	57	37	45	31
	(0.464)		(1.421)***		(1.151)	
Foreign promoters	5.50	21.20	0.00	16.00	8.10	17.90
	(−1.299)		(−1.498)		(−0.881)	
Non-promoter institutions	19	16	14	9	23	13
	(0.667)		(0.856)		(1.393)***	
Non-promoter mutual funds/UTI	3	4	1	3	3	2
	(−0.763)		(−0.877)		(0.166)	
Non-promoter banks, FIs and insurance companies	7	4	5	2	8	2
	(1.906)**		(1.526)***		(2.277)**	
Non-promoter FIIs	9	8	8	5	13	9
	(0.233)		(0.792)		(0.673)	
Based on percentage of PAT spent						
Promoters	54	59	61	47	63	50
	(−0.94)		(1.9716)***		(1.12)	
Indian promoters	45	45	54	47	57	32
	(0.01)		(0.65)		(1.859)**	
Foreign promoters	9	14	8	0	6	18
	(−0.782)		(1.123)		(−0.941)	
Non-promoter institutions	19	20	18	19	20	19
	(−0.309)		(−0.102)		(0.106)	
Non-promoter mutual funds/UTI	4	6	3	3	4	3
	(−0.904)		(0.029)		(0.378)	
Non-promoter banks, FIs and insurance companies	2	3	5	1	3	5
	(−1.734)**		(0.863)		(1.027)	
Non-promoter FIIs	12	10	9	13	13	14
	(0.673)		(−0.879)		(−0.259)	

Note All the figures are in percentages. *, ** and *** indicate significance levels at 10, 5 and 1 % level respectively

Indian listed firms which comprise of Banks, Financial Institutions, Insurance companies, Mutual funds and Foreign Institutional Investors (FIIs) respectively.

The table shows the significant differences with respect to ownership concentration in the hands of promoters who are the controlling owners. More specifically, the top companies have higher concentration of ownership by controlling owners who are family members, relatives and corporations controlled by founding families. In addition, top ranked companies in general have higher ownership by institutional investors only when categorized based on actual CSR spending.

Finally, in an unreported exercise we observe that top companies ranked on percentage of CSR spending to PAT belong to industries such as steel, chemicals, electricity generation and banking and companies from industries such as drug and pharmaceuticals, media print, and diversified fall in the category of bottom spending firms.

Table 6.6 Characteristics of top and bottom ten companies based on CSR spending and percentage of PAT

Based on actual CSR spending	2010		2011		2012	
	Top	Bottom	Top	Bottom	Top	Bottom
Age (number of years)	37	31	36	42	39	50
	(0.755)		(−0.544)		(−0.839)	
Total sales (Rs. crs)	59105.64	1180.39	84135.83	1805.66	102430.85	888.91
	(1.804)**		(2.150)**		(2.122)***	
Size (log of total assets)	4.51	3.31	4.92	3.23	4.84	3.20
	(6.313)***		(9.683)***		(6.764)***	
Profitability (PBDITA/ total assets)	0.16	0.16	0.21	0.14	0.16	0.10
	(−0.039)		(2.432)**		(1.822)**	
CSR spending (Rs. crs)	107.09	0.01	182.13	0.00	203.54	0.00
	(6.462)***		(7.199)***		(3.788)***	
CSR/PAT (%)	3	0	3	0	4	0
	(4.042)***		(5.521)***		(4.424)***	
Based on Percentage of PAT Spent						
Age (number of years)	28	37	25	42	33	37
	(0.15)		(−1.41)*		(−0.36)	
Total sales (Rs. crs)	1042.11	2727.92	967.58	2158.02	5025.20	1323.70
	(−1.49)*		(−1.27)		(1.24)	
Size (log of total assets)	3.15	3.50	3.44	3.53	3.77	3.29
	(−1.75)**		−0.48		2.248**	
Profitability (PBDITA/ total assets)	0.08	0.17	0.08	0.12	0.09	0.13
	(−2.53)***		−1.43		−1.26	
CSR spending (Rs. crs)	27.49	0.01	15.93	0.01	22.55	0.00
	2.105**		3.529***		3.826***	
CSR/PAT (%)	40	0	18	0	16	0
	4.3866***		9.951***		5.991***	

Note All the numbers are sample average across 500 firms. *, ** and *** indicate significance levels at 10, 5 and 1 % level respectively

Table 6.7 List of top ten based on CSR spending and percentage of PAT

Rank	Top ten based on CSR spending		Top ten based on % of PAT	
	Company name	Rs. cr	Company name	% of PAT
	2010			
1	Reliance Industries Ltd.	206.82	Jindal Stainless Ltd.	418
2	Coal India Ltd.	158.91	Bharat Forge Ltd.	81
3	Bharat Forge Ltd.	135.26	B F Utilities Ltd.	51
4	NMDC Ltd.	134.52	Max India Ltd.	34
5	NTPC Ltd.	123.51	Monsanto India Ltd.	30
6	Indian Oil Corpn. Ltd.	75.27	GVK Power & Infrastructure Ltd.	29
7	GAIL (India) Ltd.	64.36	GMR Infrastructure Ltd.	26
8	Tech Mahindra Ltd.	61.26	KGN Industries Ltd.	18
9	Jindal Stainless Ltd.	55.50	Deepak Fertilisers and Petrochemicals Corpn. Ltd.	16
10	Jindal Steel and Power Ltd.	55.50	Sunteck Realty Ltd.	15
	2011			
1	NTPC Ltd.	288.83	KGN Industries Ltd.	34
2	Reliance Industries Ltd.	287.74	GMR Infrastructure Ltd.	19
3	Coal India Ltd.	236.99	GVK Power & Infrastructure Ltd.	18
4	Oil and Natural Gas Corpn. Ltd.	220.00	Gujarat Narmada Valley Fertilizers & Chemicals Ltd.	17
5	Indian Oil Corpn. Ltd.	213.29	Procter & Gamble Hygiene and Health Care Ltd.	16
6	Steel Authority of India Ltd.	162.27	Edelweiss Financial Services Ltd.	16
7	Axis Bank Ltd.	157.93	Cholamandalam Investment & Finance Co. Ltd.	15
8	Tata Consultancy Services Ltd.	95.63	Adani Enterprises Ltd.	15
9	Oil India Ltd.	84.00	Century Plyboards (India) Ltd.	14
10	NMDC Ltd.	74.66	Gujarat Industries Power Co. Ltd.	13
	2012			
1	Reliance Industries Ltd.	590.00	GVK Power & Infrastructure Ltd.	32
2	Coal India Ltd.	438.38	Edelweiss Financial Services Ltd.	31
3	NTPC Ltd.	175.86	GMR Infrastructure Ltd.	19
4	Indian Oil Corpn. Ltd.	157.97	SREI Infrastructure Finance Ltd.	13
5	Tata Steel Ltd.	146.00	Adani Enterprises Ltd.	13
6	Oil and Natural Gas Corpn. Ltd.	121.00	UPL Ltd.	12
7	Jaiprakash Associates Ltd.	111.28	Engineers India Ltd.	12
8	Jindal Steel and Power Ltd.	109.37	KSK Energy Ventures Ltd.	11
9	Bharti Airtel Ltd.	106.40	Birla Corporation Ltd.	11
10	Ambuja Cements Ltd.	79.14	State Trading Corpn. of India Ltd.	9

6.5.2 Firm Characteristics and CSR Spending

This section reports the comparison of top and bottom ten companies ranked as per two aforementioned criterions across various firm specific attributes such as size, age, profitability which is reported in Table 6.6. Top ranked companies are larger and more profitable. However, there is no significant difference in age of firms in general and the differences in profitability become insignificant in the later period of study just prior to the enactment of Companies Act.

6.5.3 Comparison of Top Ten Companies on CSR Spending and Percentage of PAT

This section highlights the differences in actual CSR spending and proportion of CSR as a percentage of three years PAT. Table 6.7 presents the list of top ten companies based on these two criterions. On one hand there is some consistency in terms of companies that spent large amount of funds on CSR also contributing a large proportion of their profit, on the other hand not all the companies who spend large amount spent proportionate to their profits. The Table 6.7 captures this inconsistency. Such an inconsistency may arise due to reporting of loss in any of the preceding years in sample period which is used for computing average PAT. Another interesting observation is that the distance in terms of CSR expenditure as a proportion of profits. For example, in 2010 Jindal Stainless contributed 418 % whereas the second largest contributing company Bharat Forge contributed 81 % of their profits. Since 2011 followed by the recommendation of Companies Bill this discrepancy has reduced significantly.

6.6 Conclusion

This chapter summarizes the status of CSR activities undertaken by large 500 companies before the implementation of mandatory 2 % of PAT in the New Companies Act 2013. We observe that over the last three years, the disclosure about CSR activities is significantly increasing. However, in terms of allocating the 2 % of PAT, some of the large companies lag behind. We document various sources of CSR reporting by these companies and highlight a lack of standardisation. One of the main implications that our study draws upon is a recommendation to formulate a disclosure format under which such activities are to be reported. Indian companies disclose CSR expenditure under various heads and terms, and not necessarily as "CSR Expenditure" as one category. We rely on companies' Annual Reports for its financial and other related disclosures or information on their social spending or initiatives. During this exercise, we find that different types of reporting the expenses made for social cause or for CSR by Indian companies. Specifically, we find that companies are disclosing CSR spending information on different heads like donations, charity, CSR Budget, Allocation, Reserves, Provisions, Social Welfare expenses under the section of other expenditure. Further the chapter presents trends and patterns in CSR reporting and expenditure with respect to company characteristics such as size, age, industry and shareholding pattern.

In the next chapter we address this gap by incorporating CSR reporting practices and the actual CSR spending into the modelling framework to measure CSR initiative in general.

Chapter 7
Impact of Corporate Governance on Corporate Social Responsibility in India—Empirical Analysis

7.1 Introduction

In continuation of the previous chapter on corporate social responsibility in India, this chapter further extends the discussion by investigating the determinants of CSR activities and expenditure in large Indian corporate. Unlike developed countries, India has a specific corporate governance problem of disciplining the dominant shareholder who is in control of the management and most of the times serve on the board as well. There is a growing literature on stakeholder approach, under which, CSR can be viewed as an extended model of firms' objective of shareholder wealth maximisation by employing socially responsible practices (Friedman 1970). On the theoretical side, Tirole (2001) argues that focusing on shareholder value instead of attending to stakeholders provides more focus and sharper incentives to managers, suggesting that an enlarged fiduciary duty towards stakeholders increases agency problems. In contrast, Allen et al. (2007) come to the conclusion that under certain circumstances firms concerns with the welfare of stakeholders (e.g. suppliers or employees) can be more valuable than companies which are shareholder oriented only. Jensen (2001) discusses the stakeholder and shareholder value theory and argues in favour of a single valued objective function. As the heart of shareholder value maximisation exercise is the efficient allocation of resources by the management, corporate governance practices at the firm level becomes important in understanding firms' willingness to spend on socially responsible activities as well. As there are various governance mechanisms and their predictions on management's behaviour and corporate decisions are ambiguous it becomes an empirical question to investigate how these mechanisms affect CSR at the firm level. We utilize the specific characteristics of firm level corporate governance practices to investigate whether corporate governance plays a determining role on socially responsible activities in large Indian firms.

We propose an econometric model to analyze the determinants of CSR spending, focusing specifically on the impact of firm-level corporate governance structures and mechanisms, while accounting for the endogenous nature of such spending. The study defines propensity to conduct socially responsible activities by

S.N. Bhaduri and E. Selarka, *Corporate Governance and Corporate Social Responsibility of Indian Companies*, CSR, Sustainability, Ethics & Governance,
DOI 10.1007/978-981-10-0925-9_7

looking at the actual CSR spending as well as the disclosure of the CSR activities. In contrast to the existing literature on CSR spending, our work contributes in three primary ways: First, we have made an attempt to quantify CSR activities of largest 500 Indian companies using both qualitative and quantitative information on CSR activities. This meticulous collection of information lends a strong reliability to our analysis which is usually missing in many of the existing studies. Due to the limited information most of the empirical studies have used a much smaller sample for a single time period (e.g. Khan and Atkinson 1987; Balasubramanian et al. 2005; Ahmed 2009; Anees 2012; Mishra and Suar 2010; Oana 2010; Sharma 2011; Bihari and Pradhan 2011; Nash 2012; Ramendra and Sharad 2013; Jose and Saraf 2013; Sharma and Mani 2013). Limiting time and industry variation in the data leads to survivorship bias as well as the sample selection bias. Our study provides a wider coverage in terms of large sample size with cross sectional depth across various industrial sectors and different ownership structures.

Secondly, the choice of our sample period (2009–10 to 2011–12) also adds value to the study. Incorporating the observations just prior to the amendment of the Companies Act 2013, provides a unique opportunity to analyse the CSR spending with corporate governance and other firm specific attributes in absence of regulatory arbitrage.

Thirdly, existing empirical studies that explored the determinants of CSR have used ordinary least square framework which ignores the selection bias that stems from the firm's choice to contribute to CSR or not. In contrast, we employ an estimation technique that explicitly incorporates the sample selection bias. Specifically, the study develops an ordered probit model with sample selection to empirically analyse the relationship between corporate governance characteristics and CSR activities.

The chapter is organised as follows. Next section continues with the discussion on the data and sample selection. Section three presents our research hypotheses followed by section four detailing the construction of the endogenous and exogenous variables. Section five provides the empirical methodology with econometric specification along with descriptive statistics of variables used in the model. Section six presents the results and finally, Section seven concludes the chapter.

7.2 Data and Sample Selection

We have spent a substantial amount of time in hand collecting all the relevant information from both the standalone and consolidated financial statement of our sample companies from their Annual Reports. The top 500 Indian companies are selected for the study based on their market capitalisation (2011–12) for a period of three years from 2009–10 to 2011–12, providing a total of 1500 observations. Our selection of largest 500 companies was followed from the recent act of mandating the CSR spending for the large companies. Also, the clause 49 was implemented on these companies first which provides us the availability of all the corporate governance variables as well. One of these companies was eliminated since it was incorporated in 2012, yielding a sample of 1497 observations on 499 companies. For all the three years, we carefully scrutinized these companies' annual reports, Director's Responsibility Reports, Corporate Social Responsibility Reports, Sustainability Reports, Business Responsibility Reports and disclosure on company website.

Consistent with the empirical literature, we begin with locating a few important keywords from companies' annual reports such as—corporate social responsibility, CSR spending, CSR expenditure, social responsibility, community initiatives, social initiatives, donation, political donation, charity, education, health care, environmental protection, rural development, livelihood, agriculture, village adoption, social welfare, disaster relief, sports development, arts and culture—to capture relevant information on the disclosure of CSR activities of the firms in terms of actual expenditure as well as generic information.

As the next step, each individual company's annual report is meticulously searched for aforementioned keywords, which are further classified under seven categories namely - Education; Health Care; Community Development; Environmental protection; Sports development; Disaster Relief; and preserving Heritage, Arts & Culture. These categories are chosen to maintain consistency with the Schedule VII of the Companies Act 2013 on permissible CSR activities. We document the amount spent under these categories and also record number of beneficiaries under Education, Health care and Community Development. In addition, we also collect the information about the locations where CSR programmes have been implemented. This makes our database a unique record of CSR activities of large Indian companies, comprising of both quantitative as well as qualitative information.

7.3 Hypotheses

Our main hypotheses are built on the prominent finding in the corporate governance literature that effective governance mechanisms should reduce the insiders' ability and opportunity to over-invest in CSR (Gompers et al. 2003). There are competing hypothesis justifying the role of corporate governance in affecting the propensity of CSR activities. We focus on testing these hypotheses by consider two corporate governance mechanisms ownership structure and board of directors.

The empirical and theoretical corporate finance literature stresses two fundamental functions of the board. First, the board has the duty to oversee and thus monitor managerial actions. Second, the board is supposed to advise managers in formulating a corporation's strategy. However, in the empirical literature there is disagreement as to whether boards matter for the financial performance of a company (see Bhagat and Black 2001; Hermalin and Weisbach 1991; Yermack 1996). As a result the popular view is that boards with different characteristics will take different corporate actions and decisions (see Weisbach (1988) or Coles et al. (2008) and references therein).

First hypothesis is strategic-choice hypothesis which predicts that that the higher the managerial entrenchment, the greater the propensity for the firm's engagement in CSR to receive support from social and environmental activists (Surroca and Tribó 2008). This is similar to that developed by Pagano and Volpin (2005) to find the collusion between top managers and workers to thwart the takeover threats. We employ two variables to measure insider control over the board. First is the direct control through ownership by controlling owners (promoters) and second is strategic control where CEO or managing director is also the chairman of the board (Duality1). We also define Duality2 where controlling shareholder or promoter is also a chairman of the board which ensures that the owner's control on the board is strategic. Therefore, we expect a positive association between Duality2 and CSR if strategic choice hypothesis is true. Further in an emerging market setting, where owner-managers are likely to be entrenched we would expect a significant positive association between controlling of ownership as captured by the presence of CEO-Chairman duality in the board and the CSR activities.

Second hypothesis relates to over-investment hypothesis which follows from Barnea and Rubin (2010) who consider CSR engagement as a principal-agent relation between managers and shareholders. They argue that affiliated insiders have an interest in over-investing in CSR if doing so provides private benefits of reputation building as good global citizens, possibly at the cost of shareholders. Drawing on the Harford et al. (2008) argument that value-destroying acquisitions are made by over-confident managers, if managers have tendency to over-invest in order to build their personal reputations as good citizens, one would expect a positive association between duality1 (duality2) and CSR.

The third hypothesis—monitoring by external blockholder—stems from the agency theories that argue that the pressures from external investors, such as institutional investors, are necessary to motivate managers to maximize firm value instead of pursuing managerial objectives (Allen and Gale 2001; Jensen 1986; Shleifer and Vishny 1986). Large blockholders have an incentive to monitor managers (Demsetz and Lehn 1985; Shleifer and Vishny 1986). When the corporation is also subject to discursive scrutiny by non-investing stakeholders (i.e., social or environmental activists) as well as the large shareholder, external blockholders resolve the conflict between managers and small investors (Jensen 2001; Scherer et al. 2006). Since internal monitoring mechanisms are often viewed as ineffective (Jensen 1993), the extent to which the institutional investors provide effective external monitoring of the information transparency of CSR engagement, CSR activities should be positively associated with the presence and control by these investors (Chung and Jo 1996; Demsetz and Lehn 1985; Jo and Kim 2008; Knyazeva 2007; Shleifer and Vishny 1986; Yu 2008). We use institutional investors' ownership as a proxy for external monitoring.

7.4 Construction of Variables

7.4.1 Dependent Variable

We code all the eleven variables defined earlier as a binary variable which takes a value of one for the presence of respective keywords and zero otherwise. We also compute the average of the total amount spent on CSR by each of our sample firm. To remove the scale effect, we normalize the CSR spending to a range between zero and one. Further we add the normalized CSR spending with the above eleven variables and the average actual spending (CSR). This yields the input to our dependent variable (CSRD). More specifically, Fig. 7.1 describes the construction of dependent variable (CSRD) in three distinct steps. Step 1 codes the qualitative information, step 2 codes the quantitative.

In Step1, we capture the disclosure of information on CSR activities under seven categories of specified CSR—Education, Health Care, Community Development, Environmental protection, Sports development, Disaster Relief, and preserving Heritage, Arts & Culture. We further capture the disclosure of information under three heads, the number of beneficiaries under Education, Health care and Community Development. In addition to this, we also collect the information about the locations where CSR programmes have been implemented. We code all the eleven variables as a binary variable which takes a value of one for the presence of respective keywords and zero otherwise. We finally compute an average value for all these seven parameters.

In step two, we capture the actual CSR spending in terms of the amount spent on social activities by the firms. CSR spending is recorded from the disclosure of the expenditure details in any of these terms like Donations, Political donation, Charity, Donation & Charity, CSR Spending, CSR Expenditure, CSR Allocation, CSR Reserves and CSR Provisions. We took at most care in avoiding any double counting at this stage. Further we Normalise the CSR spending by taking the maximum value for the whole sample and dividing it with each firm level CSR spending for creating a range between 0 and 1.

At final step 3, we add step one and step two for arriving an average score which makes our database a unique record of CSR activities of large Indian companies, comprising of both quantitative as well as qualitative information. This yields the input to our dependent variable (CSRD).

Finally, we have categorised this average value into four categories (0–3) based on its observed empirical distribution is given in Table 7.1.

The category "0", the minimum score, reflects no CSR spending, average ranging between 0.01 and 0.10 are coded as Low CSR Spending as category "1"; average between 0.11 and 0.49 are coded as Medium CSR Spending as category "2" and average above 0.50 is coded as High CSR Spending as category "3". These four categories of CSR spending constitute our dependent variable, CSRD.

To be intuitively consistent, we have also taken care of two special cases while categorising the companies into four groups. First, if a company disclose all the

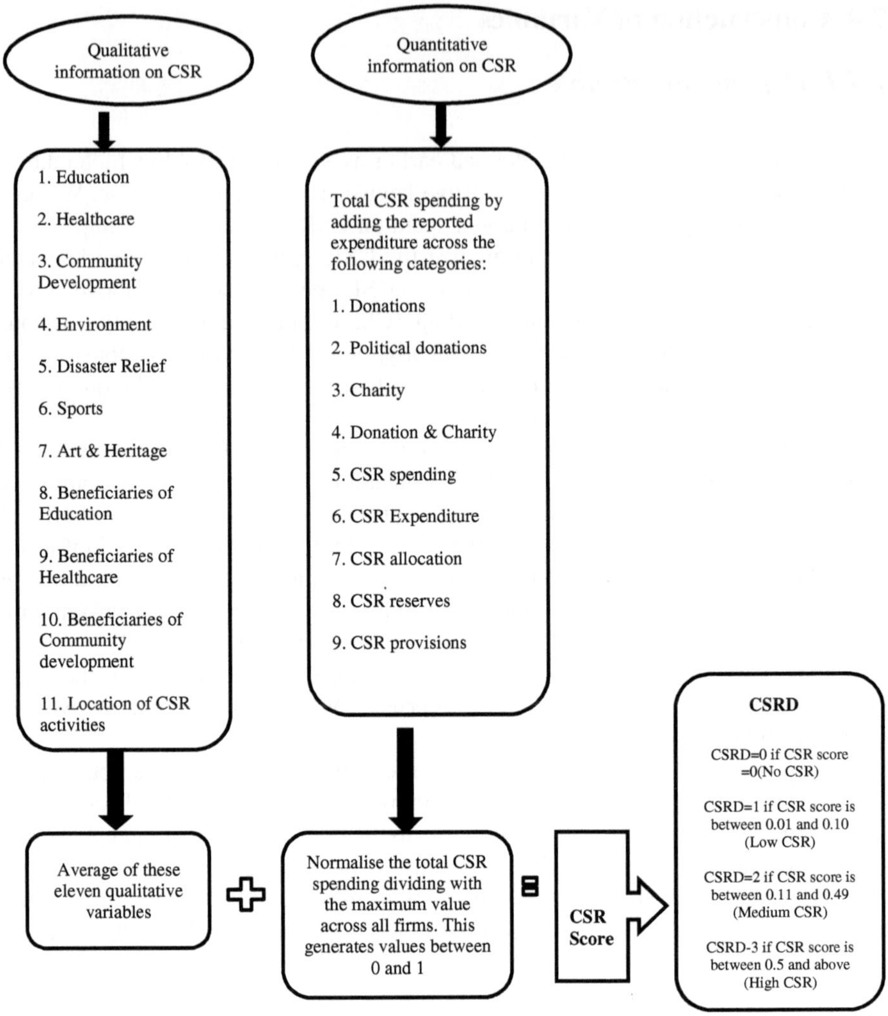

Fig. 7.1 Construction of CSRD (dependent variable)

Table 7.1 Frequency distribution of CSR

Statistics		
CSR		
Mean		0.2889
Std. deviation		0.2265
Percentiles	25	0.0900
	50	0.2800
	75	0.4500
N		1497

Source Authors compilation

qualitative information without any actual CSR spending information we assign category "0". Second, if a company reports only the CSR spending with no other qualitative information we assign category "1".

7.4.2 Explanatory Variables

Consistent with the existing literature on corporate governance and corporate social responsibility, we include a set of explanatory and control variables in our analysis. Table 7.1 provides the definition and their expected sign consistent with the existing literature.

We consider both the internal (ownership concentration and board structure) and external (institutional ownership) monitoring consistent with the corporate governance literature to capture the extent of agency problem in undertaking CSR activities by large Indian firms.

7.4.2.1 Ownership Concentration

We measure internal control in terms of promoter shareholding and external control in terms of shareholdings by institutional investors. Promoters are controlling owners and therefore the concentration of ownership in the hands of promoters is used as a proxy for insider control. The effect of insider control depends on the trade off between the alignment of interests of controlling owners with non-controlling owners and incentives to expropriation (Sarkar and Sarkar 2008; Selarka 2005; Pant and Pattanayak 2007). Following strategic choice hypothesis we expect a positive association between promoter ownership and CSR activities.

Institutional ownership is proportion of ownership held by domestic institutional investors such as mutual funds, banks, financial institutions and insurance companies. These institutions may exert a pressure to utilize the resources after operations to reduce the managerial entrenchment on free cash flow. At the same time, these investors are embedded in the society to encourage socially responsible behaviour by firms. If external block holder hypothesis is true, we would expect a positive association between institutional ownership and CSR. Following the external blockholder hypothesis, we expect a positive association between institutional investor ownership and CSR.

7.4.2.2 Board of Directors

Board size: With respect to the board size, various studies, such as those by Yermack (1996), Eisenberg et al. (1998) and De Andrés et al. (2005), find that the presence of a larger number of board members translates into lower (board) efficiency when the Board monitors the management, as a result of an increase in agency problems. A reduction in board efficiency could lead to a lesser predisposition to disclose information about the company's activities, whether owing to a lack of suitable control mechanisms or the need to conceal bad or non-optimal news from shareholders. Furthermore, the complexity of management control and the truthfulness of the information require a considerable number of board members with the necessary experience and diversity to correctly perform such monitoring duties (Bradbury 1990). In this sense, a larger Board would perform better monitoring, which would translate into the dissemination of greater volumes of information. Karamanou and Vafeas (2005) and Cheng and Courtenay (2006) have found no relationship between the size of the Board of Directors and the dissemination of information, whereas Gallego (2006) evidence a positive effect. Under strategic-choice hypothesis we expect a positive association between board size and propensity of CSR activities. Under the over-investment hypothesis, as the members of the board may side with the CEO, there could be a negative effect on CSR.

Board independence: We measure board independence in terms of proportion of independent directors on the board. A company's reputation is stronger if the Board of Directors has a large number of nonexecutive members because, as posited by Zahra and Stanton (1988), these types of board members are those who are most interested in demonstrating compliance with regulations and responsible behaviour by the entity. Ibrahim and Angelidis (1995) affirm that non-executive board members are assumed to be more sensitive to social demands, finding themselves in a better position than executive board members to protect the interests of the stakeholder. With the exception of the papers by Lim et al. (2007) and Haniflä and Cooke (2005), the results of other previous studies confirm the existence of a positive relationship between the presence of nonexecutive board members and aspects such as the socially responsible behaviour of the company (O'Neill et al. 1989), the amount of financial information disseminated (Chen and Jaggi 2001; Willekens et al. 2005), the quality level of the information (Karamanou and Vafeas 2005) and the dissemination of voluntary information, whether general (Cheng and Courtenay 2006) or specific to CSR (Barako and Brown 2008; Prado-Lorenzo et al. 2009), as well as the adoption of codes of ethics (García Sánchez et al. 2011; Rodriguez-Dominguez et al. 2009). We expect a positive relationship between the board independence and CSR.

Insider controlled board: Insiders can have operational, strategic or both types of control by having a position on the board. We define insider control on board in terms of two dummy variables. First is, if the CEO/MD is also the chairman of the board (Duality 1). Second, if the promoter is a CEO/MD or the chairman of the board (Duality2). Under strategic choice and over-investment hypotheses we expect a positive significant coefficient for these variables.

7.4.2.3 Control Variables

Size: Existing literature has offered a number of interpretations of company size as determinant of CSR that ranges from organisational visibility to market power. Larger companies are likely to invest more in CSR given their large consumer base and access to the large financial resources (Meznar et al. 1994; Roberts 1992;

Cowen et al. 1987; Ball and Foster 1982). As in Lenway and Rehbein (1991), we measure company size as the natural logarithm of total value of asset. We expect a positive association between company size and social expenditure.

Profitability: Existing literature has argued that financial performance of a company is recognised as a potential influence on social spending as profitable companies are likely to have the discretionary funds to commit to other programmes whereas companies with poor financial performance are likely to restrict socially responsible expenditures (Navarro 1988; Siegfried et al. 1983; Adams and Hardwick 1998; Roberts 1992). We measure profitability as ratio of net profit earned before depreciation, interest and taxes to total assets.

Dividend: As dividend paying companies are generally are better performing companies, we expect a positive association between dividend payout and CSR. Also, the corporate finance literature often uses dividend payout as a signal for better financial health of a company.

Age: Previous research (Cormier et al. 2005; Roberts 1992; Jiraporn and Chintrakarn 2013) has established that the age of a company influences the CSR activities undertaken by the firm. We hypothesize that age and the CSR are positively correlated suggesting long established firms tend to contribute more towards socially responsible activities. Natural logarithm of number of years since incorporation has been used as a proxy for Age.

Finally, Table 7.2 provides the details of the construction of independent variables with their definition, expected sign and the supporting literature.

7.4.3 Stylized Facts in CSR

To have a preliminary insight into the interaction between CSR Spending and other firm related attributes, we have looked into a series of graphs presented in Fig. 7.2a–c respectively. Some of the preliminary trends from the graphs indicate that:

- Larger the company size higher the CSR Spending.
- Profitable companies are associated with highest level of CSR spending.
- Firms with large boards spend more.
- There is a positive association between the proportion of independent directors and CSR.
- Except for the year 2011, the ownership concentration in the hands of promoters is associated with higher CSR spending.
- Leverage and CSR spending is negatively correlated.
- Duality 1 and Duality 2 show a positive association with CSR.
- Majority of "no CSR" firms belong to Banking Industry and "high CSR" firms belong to Chemicals.

As indicated in Fig. 7.2c, with respect to the ownership structure, eye balling of the data shows that the business groups dominate across all the four categories which is a sample related feature as majority of our sample consists of firms belonging to business groups.

Table 7.2 Description of variables

Variables	Variable definition	Expected sign	Supporting literature
Size (S)	Natural logarithm of total assets	(+)	Dierkes and Preston (1977), Patten (1991), Roberts (1992), Hackston and Milne (1996), Adams and Hardwick (1998), Brammer and Millington (2006), Aras et al. (2010), Siregar and Bachtiar (2010), Jiraporn and Chintratarn (2013), Kansal et al. (2014)
Profitability (P)	Earnings Before Depreciation, Interest and Taxes (EBDIT) divided by total assets	(+)	Ullmann (1985), McGuire et al. (1988), Roberts (1992), Waddock and Gravess (1997), Adams and Hardwick (1998), Brammer and Millington (2006), Aras et al. (2010), Crisostomo et al. (2011), Jiraporn and Chintratarn (2013), Kansal et al. (2014)
Age (AGE)	Natural logarithm of current year minus year of incorporation	(+)	Roberts (1992), Cormier et al. (2005), Kansal et al. (2014)
Board Size (BS and BSQ)	Natural logarithm of total number of directors on board. (natural logarithm of the square of total number of directors)	(?)	Ho and Wong (2001), Eng and Mak (2003), Gul and Leung (2004), Barako et al. (2006), Hossain and Reaz (2007), Huafang and Jianguo (2007), Li et al. (2008), Akhtaruddin et al. (2009)
Proportion of Independent Directors (PROID)	Total number of Independent Directors divided by Board size	(+)	Cheng and Jaggi (2000), Cheng and Courtenay (2006), Barako et al. (2006), Patelli and Prencipe (2007)
Dividend Payout (DIV)	Dummy variable = 1 if the company has paid dividend; 0 otherwise	(+)	Fama and French (2001), Von Eije and Megginson (2008), Goss and Roberts (2011)
Promoters Control (PROM)	Dummy variable = 1 if total promoters share >60 %; 0 Otherwise	(+)	Jensen and Meckling (1976), Ullmann (1985), Haley (1991), Roberts (1992), Adams and Hardwick (1998)
Duality 1	Dummy variable = 1 if CEO/MD is also the Chairman of the board; 0 otherwise	(+)	Gompers et al. (2003), Pagano and Volpin (2005), Surroca and Tribo (2008), Barnea and Rubin (2010)
Duality 2	Dummy variable = 1 if Chairman of the board is a Promoter; 0 otherwise	(+)	Gompers et al. (2003), Pagano and Volpin (2005), Surroca and Tribo (2008), Barnea and Rubin (2010)

Source Authors compilation

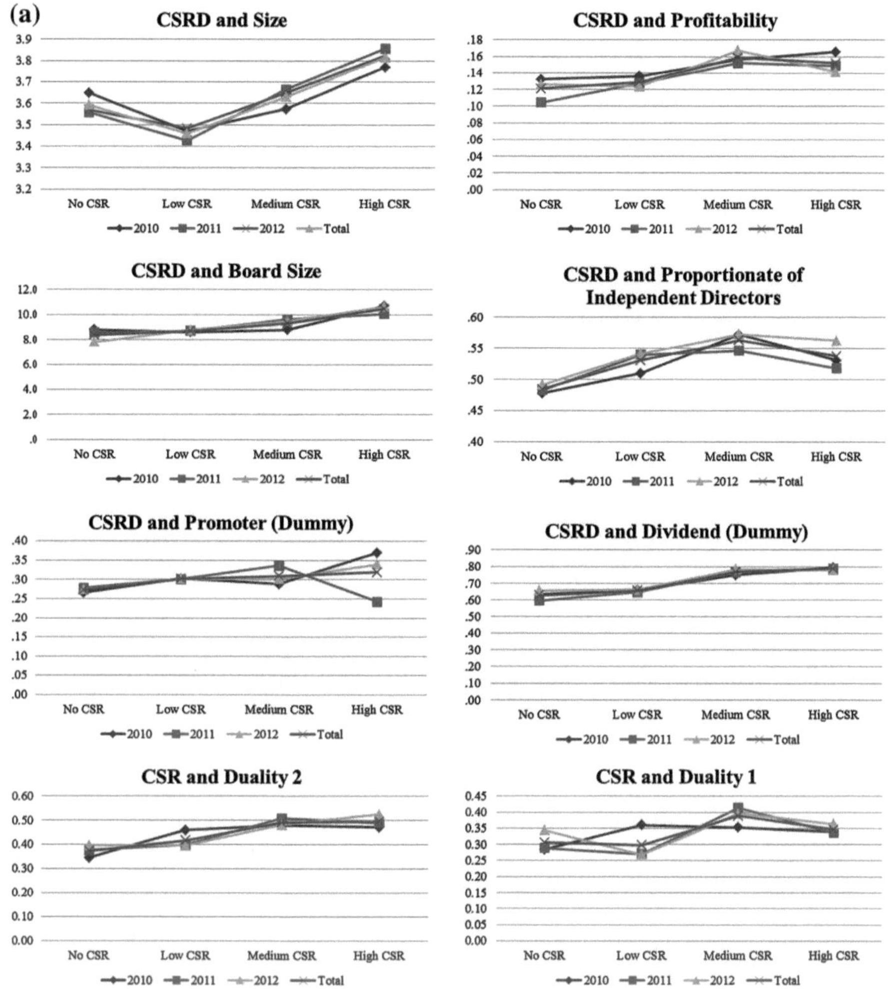

Fig. 7.2 **a** Interaction of CSRD with explanatory variables. **b** Distribution of CSRD across industries. **c** Distribution of CSRD by ownership structure

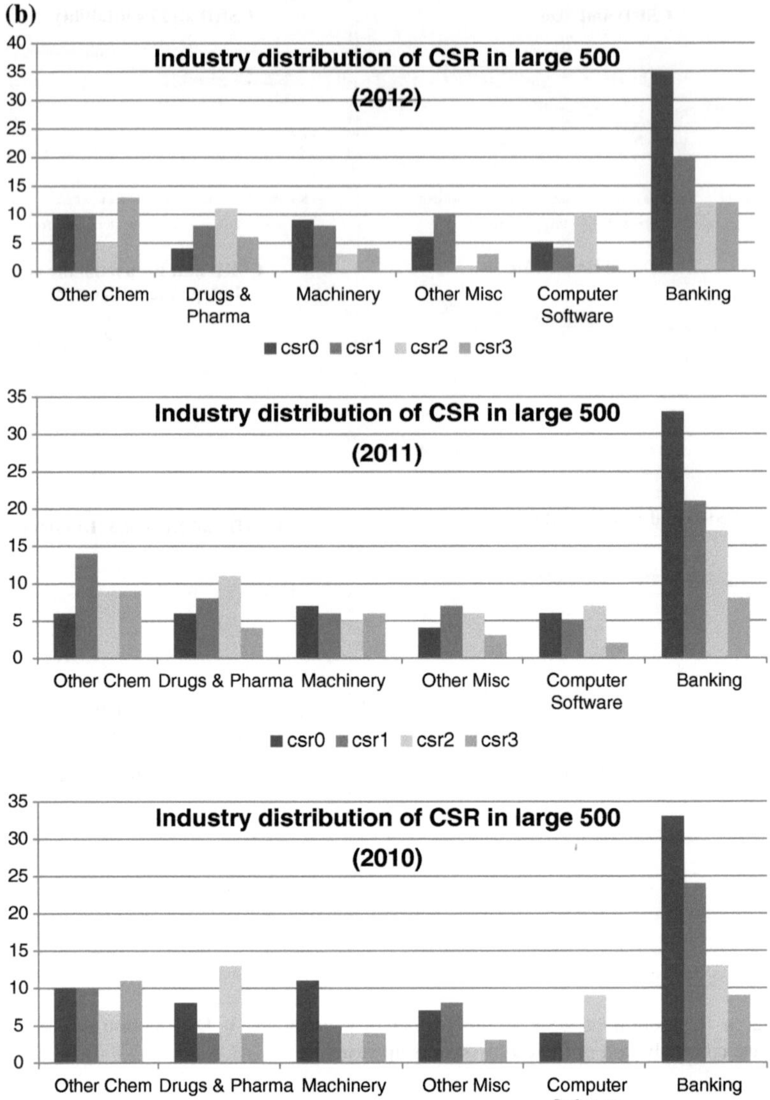

Fig. 7.2 (continued)

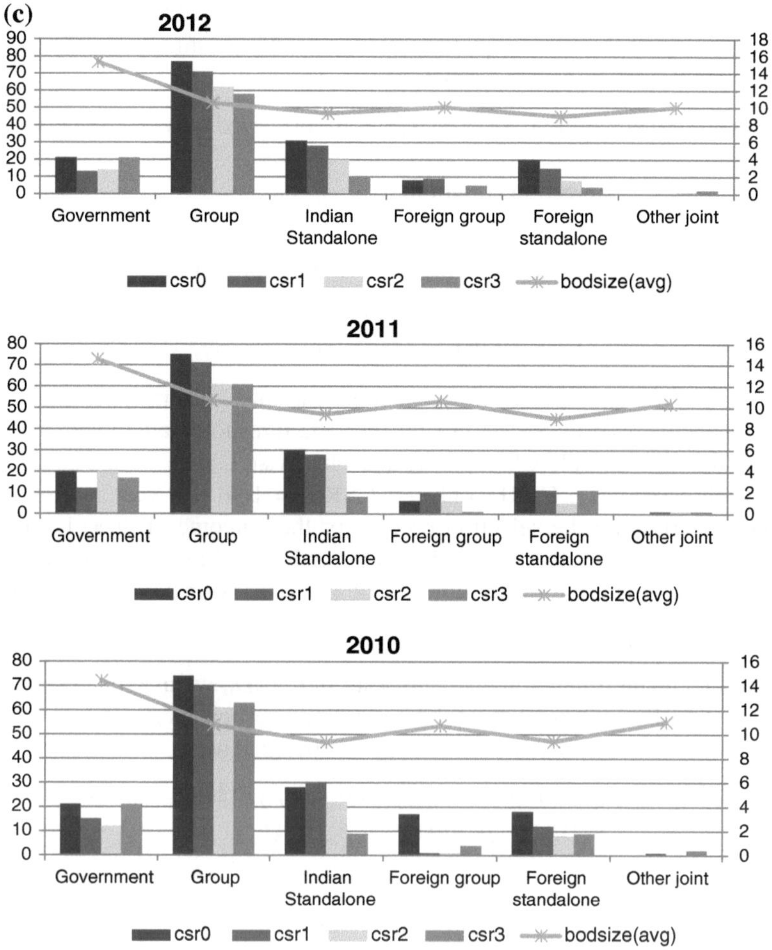

Fig. 7.2 (continued)

7.5 Empirical Methodology

As mentioned earlier, most of the empirical studies that have explored the determinants and dynamics of CSR have deployed naive ordinary least square based models by completely ignoring the selectivity bias that may be inevitable in many observational studies like ours. To address this, we have proposed an alternative empirical specification using Heckman's ordered probit model with sample selection. This specification explicitly addresses the sample selection bias emanating from the companies' choice to contribute and disclose CSR information or not.

Typically a sample selection model (Heckman 1978, 1979) involves two equations: The regression equation that explains the variation in dependent variable and the selection equation considering a portion of the sample whose outcome is observed and mechanisms that determines the selection process. Next we describe the construction of these two equations along with their estimation process. As for any selection model, ours also consists of two equations:

$$\text{Regression equation: } \mathrm{CSRD_i} = \mathrm{x_1}\beta + \mu_\mathrm{i}, \text{observed only if } \mathrm{CSRD_i} = 1,$$

$$\begin{aligned} &\text{Selection equation:} \\ &\mathrm{CSRS_i} = z_i\lambda + \varepsilon_i, \\ &\mathrm{CSRS_i} = 1 \text{ if } \mathrm{CSRS_i^*} > 0;\ 0 \text{ otherwise} \\ &\mathrm{Prob}(CSRD_i = 1|z_i) = \Phi(z_i\gamma) \quad \text{and} \\ &\mathrm{Prob}(CSRD_i = 0|z_i) = 1 - \Phi(z_i\gamma) \end{aligned}$$

where $\mathrm{x_i}$ and $\mathrm{z_i}$ are vector of exogenous variables determining $\mathrm{CSRD_i}$ and $\mathrm{CSRS_i}$ respectively. If $\mathrm{CSRS_i^*}$ is greater than the threshold value (say 0), then the observed dummy variable $\mathrm{CSRS_i} = 1$, and otherwise $\mathrm{CSRS_i} = 0$. The regression equation observes value $\mathrm{CSRD_i}$ only for $\mathrm{CSRS_i} = 1$; $\mathrm{z_i}$ is a vector of exogenous variables determining the selection process or the outcome of $\Phi(\bullet)$ is the standard normal cumulative distribution function; and ε_1 and ε_2 are error terms of the two regression equations, and assumed to be bivariate normal, with mean zero and covariance matrix $\begin{bmatrix} \sigma_\varepsilon & \rho \\ \rho & 1 \end{bmatrix}$.

Given incidental truncation and censoring of $\mathrm{CSRD_i}$, we use the observed variables (i.e., CSRD, x, z) to estimate the regression coefficients β and λ.

Specifically the regression equation can be specified as:

$$\begin{aligned} CSRD_i = \alpha_i, &+\beta_1 S_i + \beta_2 P_i + \beta_3 \ln BS_i + \beta_4 \ln BSQ_i + \beta_5 PROID_i \\ &+ \beta_6 DIV_i + \beta_7 PROM_i + \beta_8 DUAL_i + \mu_i \end{aligned}$$

where

CSRD = categorical variable taking values from 0 to 3
$\mathrm{S_i}$ = Size
P = Profitability
BS = Natural Logarithm of Board size
BSQ = Natural Logarithm of Board size Square
PROID = Proportion of Independent directors
DIV = Dividend paid (Dummy)
PROM = Percentage of Promoters Shares Held (Dummy)
DUAL = Duality1/Duality 2 (Dummy)
μ_i = is the error term of the equation.

The selection equation is:

$$CSRS_\mathrm{i}^* = \alpha_i + z_i\lambda + \varepsilon_i, \quad \mathrm{CSRS_i} = 1 \text{ if } \mathrm{CSRS_i^*} > 0, \text{ and } \mathrm{CSRS_i} = 0 \text{ otherwise}$$

The estimation equation is:

$$CSRS_i = \alpha_i, +\gamma_1 AGE_i + \gamma_2 P_i + \gamma_3 DIV_i + \gamma_4 PROM_i + \gamma_5 IINV_i + \varepsilon_i$$

where

CSRS = the CSR spending Dummy variables takes value = 1 if CSRD > 0
P = Profitability
AGE = Natural Logarithm of Age
DIV = Dividend paid (Dummy) and
PROM = Percentage of Promoters Shares Held (Dummy)
IINV = Institutional investors' ownership
ε_i = is the error term of the equation.

In our case, the selection equation indicates that the CSR spending is observed only for those companies whose CSR spending were greater than 0 (i.e., companies were considered as having spending for CSR if and only if their CSR spending was above a certain threshold value). Using a zero value in this equation is a normalization convenience and is an alternate way to say that the companies who contributed for CSR was greater than their counterparts (i.e., CSRS > CSRS*). The selection model further assumes that μ_i and ε_i are correlated.

7.5.1 Ordered Probit with Sample Selection

Since our dependent variable is a categorical variable we use an ordered probit model with sample selection. Following De Luca and Perotti (2011), the maximum likelihood estimator used for our model is as follows:

$$y_j = \sum_{h=1}^{H} v_h 1(k_{h-1} < X_j\beta + u_{1j} \leq k_h)$$

where X_j is the outcome covariates, β is the coefficients, and u_{1j} is a random-error term. The observed outcome values $v_1,\ldots,v_H$ are integers such that $v_i < v_m$ for $i < m$. $K_1,\ldots,k_{H-1}$ are real numbers such that $k_i < k_m$ for $i < m$, k_0 is taken as $-\infty$ and k_H is taken as $+\infty$.

The probability that the ordinal outcome y_j is equal to the value v_h is given by the probability that $X_j\beta + u_{1j}$ falls within the cut-off points k_{h-1} and k_h,

$$\Pr(y_j = v_h) = \Pr(k_{h-1} < X_j\beta + u_{1j} \leq k_h)$$

We model the selection process for the outcome by the selection equation as:

$$s_j = 1\,(z_j\gamma + u_{2j} > 0)$$

where $s_j = 1$ if we observed y_j and 0 otherwise, z_j is the covariates used to model the selection process, γ is the coefficients for the selection process, $1(\cdot)$ denotes the indicator function, and u_{2j} is a random-error term.

(u_{1j}, u_{2j}) have bivariate normal distribution with mean zero and variance matrix

$$\begin{bmatrix} 1 & \rho \\ \rho & 1 \end{bmatrix}$$

When $\rho \neq 0$, standard ordered probit techniques applied to the outcome equation yield inconsistent results.

The probability of selection is $\Pr(s_j = 1) = \Phi(z_j\gamma + \text{offset}_j^\gamma)$ where $\Phi_2(\cdot)$ is the standard cumulative normal distribution function. The probability of selection and the outcome $y_j = v_h$ is

$$\Pr(y_j = v_h, s_j = 1) = \Phi_2(z_j\gamma + \text{offset}_j^\gamma, k_h - x_j\beta - \text{offset}_j^\beta, -\rho) - \Phi_2(z_j\gamma + \text{offset}_j^\gamma, k_{h-1} - x_j\beta - \text{offset}_j^\beta, -\rho)$$

$\Phi_2(\cdot)$ is the standard cumulative bivariate normal distribution function (with mean [o o]').

The probability of selection and the outcome $y_j = v_h$ is

$$\Pr(y_j = v_h, s_j = 0) = \Phi_2(-z_j\gamma + \text{offset}_j^\gamma, k_h - x_j\beta - \text{offset}_j^\beta, -\rho) - \Phi_2(-z_j\gamma + \text{offset}_j^\gamma, k_{h-1} - x_j\beta - \text{offset}_j^\beta, -\rho)$$

Let $a_j = z_j\gamma + \text{offset}_j^\gamma$ and $b_j = x_j\beta + \text{offset}_j^\beta$. This yields the log likelihood

$$\ln L = \sum_{j \notin S} w_j \ln\{\Phi(-a_j)\} + \sum_{h=1}^{H} \sum_{\substack{j \notin S \\ y_j = v_h}} w_j \ln\{\Phi_2(a_j, k_h - b_j, -\rho) - \Phi_2(a_j, k_{h-1} - b_j, -\rho)\}$$

where S is the set of observations for which y_j is observed, $\Phi_2(\cdot)$ is the cumulative bivariate normal distribution function (with mean [0 0]'), $\Phi_2(\cdot)$ is the standard cumulative normal, and w_j is an optional weight for observation j.

The probability of outcome $y_j = v_j$ given selection is

$$\Pr(y_j = v_h, |s_j = 1 = \frac{\Pr(y_j = v_h, s_j = 1)}{\Pr(s_j = 1)}$$

The probability of outcome $y_j = v_j$ given y_j is not selection is

$$\Pr(y_j = v_h, |s_j = 0 = \frac{\Pr(y_j = v_h, s_j = 0)}{\Pr(s_j = 0)}$$

The marginal probabilities of the outcome y_j are

$$\Pr(y_j = v_1) = \Phi(k_1 - x_j\beta - \text{offset}_j^\beta)$$

$$\Pr(y_j = v_H) = 1 - \Phi(k_{H-1} - x_j\beta - \text{offset}_j^\beta)$$

$$\Pr(y_j = v_h) = \Phi(k_h - x_j\beta - \text{offset}_j^\beta) - \Phi(k_{h-1} - x_j\beta - \text{offset}_j^\beta)$$

7.5.2 Descriptive Statistics

This section provides the descriptive statistics of the variables used in the model. The distribution of outcome variable (CSRD) is shown in Fig. 7.2 for the full sample. For each time period the same figure is presented in the Annexure.

The distribution of CSRD reveals that 31 % of the sample fall in the Category 0 indicating that majority of firms are neither spending nor disclosing about CSR activities. The higher proportion of firms falling in this category justifies our choice of empirical model which corrects for sample selection bias arising from the fact that large numbers of firms in our sample do not report any information on CSR. Around 20 % of the sample fall into the Category 3, 22 % are falling into the Category 2 and 27 % are falling into the Category 1 respectively.

We also report the distribution of the outcome variable across sample period in the Table 7.3. We observe that there is a transition of companies across these categories over the sample period. Specifically, the percentage of firms under lower CSR spending has increased compared to the firms with high CSR spending.

Finally, Table 7.4 describes the descriptive statistics of the variables used in our empirical analysis.

Table 7.3 Number of companies reported in each category of CSRD

CSRD/Year	2010	2011	2012	Total
No CSR	158 (32)	151(30)	157 (31)	466 (31)
Low CSR	129 (26)	133 (27)	136 (27)	398 (27)
Medium CSR	104 (21)	116 23)	106 (22)	326 (22)
High CSR	108 (22)	99 (20)	100 (20)	307 (21)
Total	499 (100)	499 (100)	499 (100)	1497 (100)

Source Authors compilation
Note Figures in parentheses are percentages

Table 7.4 Descriptive statistics of variables used in the model

Variable	Mean	Std. dev.
CSRD (average value)	0.2889	0.2265
Size (total assets in Rs. crore)	21,884.49	74,517.32
Profitability (Rs. in crore)	2058.06	5764.50
Age (number of years)	38	27.34
Board size (number)	9	4.36
Board size square (number)	18	8.73
Proportion of independent directors (%)	0.5640	0.2247
Promoters (%)	48.8	25.46
Dividend dummy	0.7	0.46
Promoter dummy	0.3	0.46
Institutional Investors ownership (%)	21.8	14.74
Duality1 dummy	0.33	0.47
Duality2 dummy	0.44	0.50

Source Authors' compilation

7.6 Discussion of Results

The results for different model specifications are reported in Table 7.5.

The selection model reveals that the firm's decision to contribute to CSR or not is significantly determined by its Age, Profitability, Dividend, and the extent of Promoter control. More specifically we find that younger and less financially constrained firms are more likely to spend in CSR than the older and more financially

Table 7.5 Results of ordered probit selection model

Independent variables	Model 1	Model 2	Model 3	Model 4	Model 5
Size (S)	0.2348*	0.2501**	0.267*	0.2418*	0.2724*
Profitability (P)	1.1690*	0.6919	0.7718	0.7219	0.7401
Board size (BS)	−0.3906**	−0.2713	−0.18163	−0.25099	0.0366
Board size square (BSQ)	0.1408**	0.1013	0.0724	0.0921	–
Board independence (PROID)	0.2269	0.2011	0.00122	0.1793	0.0429
Dividend (DIV)	0.2569*	0.2812*	0.2626*	0.2811*	0.2286*
Promoter (PROM)	0.2878*	0.3108*	0.3153*	0 .304*	0.2920*
Institutional investor ownership (IINV)	0.0104	0.0119*	0.0127*	0.0127*	0.0146*
Duality1 (D)	–	–	−0.0468	–	–
Duality2 (D)	–	–	0.2395**	0.1602**	0.1965*
Ownership	–	–	Yes	–	Yes
Industry (D)	–	Yes	Yes	Yes	Yes
Selection model					
AGE	−0.0994**	−0.1052**	−0.1042**	−0.1021**	−0.1630*
Profitability	0.7702**	0.7957**	0.80626**	0.7965**	0.8280**
Dividend (D)	0.3046*	0.3079*	0.3122*	0.3121*	0.2469*
Promoter (D)	0.1468***	0.1488***	0.1576**	0.1581**	0.1617***
Institutional investor ownership (IINV)	0.000001	0.00005	0.0003	0.00032	0.0032
Ownership (D)	–	–	–	–	Yes
Industry (D)	–	Yes	Yes	Yes	Yes
Constant	0.4425*	0.4615*	0.4393**	0.4333**	1.2829*
Cut1	1.5780*	1.4321*	1.623*	1.474*	1.4419*
Cut2	2.3280*	2.2532*	2.4611*	2.299*	2.2983*
Wald X^2	83.10*	92.58*	100.55*	93.68*	163.08*
Prob > X^2	0.000	0.000	0.001	0.000	0.000
Pseudo R^2	0.0611	0.085	0.092	0.090	0.122
Log likelihood	−1928.726	−1878.021	−1864.07	−1867.687	−1804.43
LR test (Rho)	0.72***	0.65***	0.63***	0.65***	0.59***
Prob > X^2	0.051	0.089	0.098	0.096	0.074

Note Significance level: ***$p < 0.1$; **$p < 0.05$; *$p < 0.01$ (*D*—dummy variables)

constrained firms. Consistent with our survey of case studies and anecdotal evidences, firms with concentrated ownership structure which are either part of business groups or government controlled in our sample, are more likely to spend on CSR compared to firms which are widely held.

Among all the competing models, model 5 turns out to be most parsimonious one with the highest pseudo R^2 of 0.122 and the highest Wald test suggesting overall goodness of fit. Further the LR Test of independent equations (Rho) is also significant at 10 % level justifying our selection of Ordered Probit with Sample Selection model over the simple Ordered Probit Model.

After controlling for the sample selection model, our results are consistent with the theoretical predictions about size and dividend payout. In addition, concentrated ownership in the hands of controlling owners positively influences the probability of higher CSR activities. This is also consistent after controlling for ownership groups and industries where firms are operating into. Positive and significant effect of Promoter control and Duality2 support the strategic choice and over-investment hypotheses. However, we do not find significant effect of Duality 1 when we include Duality2 in the model. Given the history of political connectedness of family-owned management in India since pre-independence, the strategic choice hypothesis provides an appropriate explanation of higher CSR activities by owner-controlled firms and owner controlled boards. These owner-directors are usually associated with the companies since inception and might have higher commitment towards society. This argument is consistent with the research in sociology and organizational behaviour, suggesting that organizational commitment increases with tenure and directors with higher tenure might work harder because they have a more pronounced long term interest in the success of the firm and care about the wellbeing of employees. However, we cannot establish this argument because employee related activities are not being considered as CSR in our study following the Companies Act 2013 unlike the studies from the developed countries.

Positive and significant coefficient, consistent with the existing literature, on institutional investors' ownership plays an important role in explaining CSR activities for the Indian firms. This is consistent with our external blockholder hypothesis.

To check the consistency and robustness of our findings, we report the distribution of the estimated scores from the regression model (Model 5) in Table 7.6 and Fig. 7.3 respectively. The highest average score for the Category 3 and lowest average score for the Category 0 suggest a consistent fit of the model.

Table 7.6 Distribution of estimated score for the dependent variable

CSRD	Mean score
Low disclosure	1.1027
Medium disclosure	1.5463
High disclosure	1.8748
Total	1.4778

Source Authors compilation

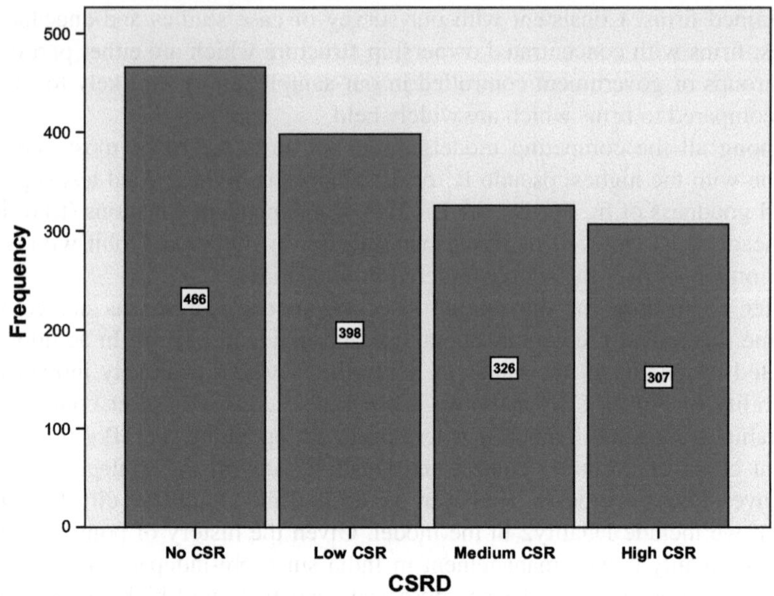

Fig. 7.3 Frequency distribution of dependent variable (CSRD)

The distribution shown in the Fig. 7.3 clearly demonstrate a monotonically increasing score for CSR across the various categories indicating the ability of our model to capture the extent of CSR spending across various groups.

7.6.1 Marginal Effects and Predicted Probabilities

Since one of our primary objective is to explore the convergence of corporate governance and corporate social responsibility spending we have evaluated the marginal effects and predicted probabilities for the corporate governance variables included in Model 5 after holding all other variables at their mean levels. These results are reported in Table 7.7 and in Fig. 7.4 respectively.

The predicted probabilities are considerably lower for the firms where Chairman or CEO belongs to the Promoter group (Duality 2) for lower range of CSR spending and considerably higher for the middle and higher ranges of CSR spending. Similarly for the firms with a concentrated promoter shares held tend to spend more on CSR. Government firms tend to spend more on CSR compared to the Indian Business groups as well as standalone. On the other hand, Indian standalone firms tend to spend much less on CSR than that of their foreign counterparts (Fig. 7.5).

Table 7.7 Marginal and predicted probabilities

	Predicted probabilities for low CSR	Predicted probabilities for medium CSR	Predicted probabilities for high CSR
Duality2 = 0	0.54	0.29	0.17
Duality2 = 1	0.47	0.31	0.22
Promoter = 0	0.55	0.29	0.17
Promoter = 1	0.43	0.32	0.25
Government owned	0.49	0.31	0.21
Indian Business Groups	0.50	0.31	0.20
Indian standalone	0.55	0.29	0.16
Foreign Business Groups	0.65	0.24	0.11
Foreign standalone	0.48	0.31	0.21

Source Authors' compilation

Fig. 7.4 Distribution of estimated score values for the outcome variable

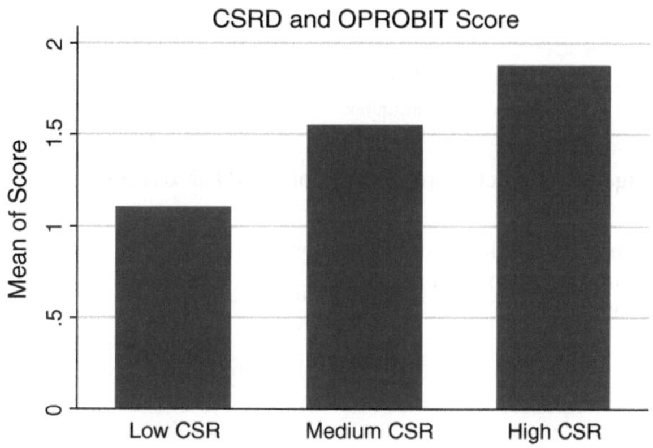

7.6.2 Data Validation for Non-sample Companies

In order to check the validation and robustness of our model we have also carried out an out of sample validation exercises using 50 companies randomly selected from the Top 1000 Indian firms excluding our sample companies. The validation results are presented in Table 7.8 and Fig. 7.6. The results reveal a similar monotonically increasing score across various categories, clearly demonstrating the robustness of our findings even for the out of sample firms.

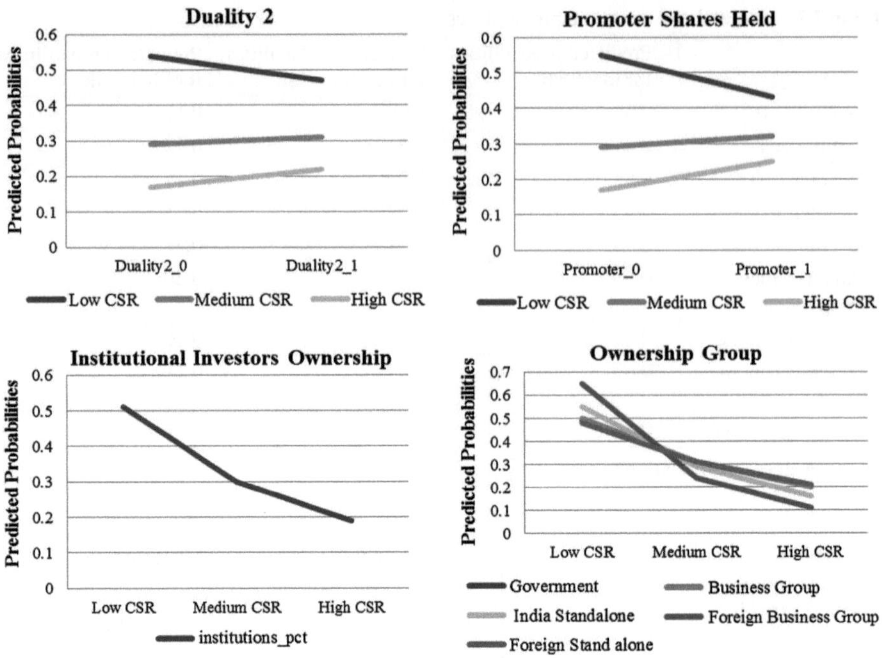

Fig. 7.5 Predicted probabilities of CSRD across corporate governance characteristics

Table 7.8 Validation score results for out of sample companies

CSRD	Mean score
No CSR	1.1648
Low CSR	1.3449
Medium CSR	1.5329
Total	1.2238

Source Authors' compilation

Fig. 7.6 Validation score results for out of sample companies. *Source* Authors' compilation from estimation results

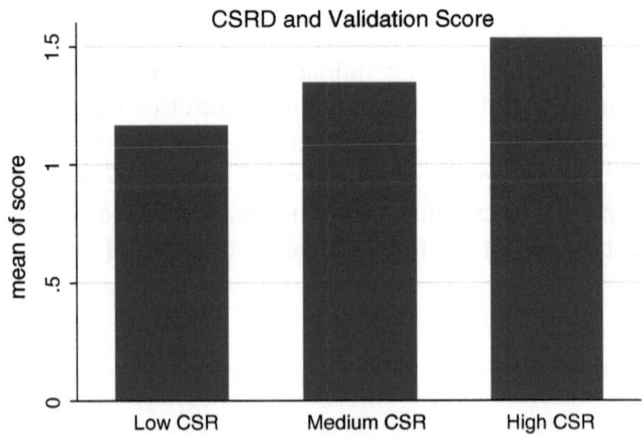

7.7 Conclusion

This study makes significant contribution to the literature by analysing the role of corporate governance in terms of ownership structure and board of directors on socially responsible practices in large Indian firms. Our estimation methodology controls for the sample selection as in absence of regulatory compliance, many of the firms do not report amount spent on CSR and report disclosure of CSR activities instead.

We find that firms which are older, larger and pay dividend are more likely to undertake the CSR activities. We also find significant positive relationship between CSR and proportion of controlling shareholders which implies that founding families or government are driven by strategic decision of investing into CSR related activities. This is also in line with the positive relationship between insiders' control over board and CSR. In contrast, fraction of independent directors does not affect the CSR even though our univariate analysis suggests that firms with higher proportion of independent directors spend more on CSR activities.

To our surprise, profitability does not have any significant relationship with CSR activities. This questions the recent mandate of diverting 2 % of the profit towards CSR activities in the Companies Act 2013. It is worth noting that some of the puzzling results presented in this section could be due to the unobservable nature of our attributes such as corporate governance along with the inaccurate measurement of the proxies to capture these attributes. We attempt to address some of these challenges in the following chapter by developing a structural equation model.

Further, the results are robust to the out of sample validation. We also develop robust methodology to predict the propensity of CSR activities that are likely to be undertaken by the firms based on four categories—no, low, medium and high CSR—respectively. This method is tested and validated for a random sample of fifty companies that are not part of our sample.

References

Adams M, Hardwick P (1998) An analysis of corporate donations: United Kingdom evidence. J Manage Stud 35(5):641–654

Ahmed N (2009) ASSOCHAM eco pulse study: corporate social responsibility 2008-09. ASSOCHAM Research Bureau

Akhtaruddin M, Hossain MA, Hossain M, Yao L (2009) Corporate governance and voluntary disclosure in corporate annual reports of malaysian listed firms. J Appl Manag Account Res 7(1):1–20

Allen F, Carletti E, Marquez R (2007) Stakeholder capitalism, corporate governance and firm value, Working Paper, University of Pennsylvania

Allen F, Gale D (2001) Comparing financial systems. Cambridge, Massachusetts: The MIT Press

Anees M (2012) Corporate social responsibility in India based on NSE NIFTY Companies. Int J Market Financ Serv Manage Res 1(12):70–79

Aras G, Aybars A, Kutlu O (2010) Managing corporate performance Investigating the relationship between corporate social responsibility and financial performance in emerging markets, Int J Prod Perf Manag 59(3):229–254

Balasubramanian NK, Kimber D, Siemensma F (2005) Emerging opportunities or traditions reinforced. J Corp Citizenship 2005(17):79–92

Ball R, Foster G (1982) Corporate financial reporting: a methodological review of empirical research, Studies on current research methodologies in accounting: a critical evaluation, supplement to vol. 20 of journal of accounting research, pp 161–234

Barako DG, Brown AM (2008) Corporate social reporting and board representation: evidence from the Kenyan banking sector. J Manage Gov 12(4):309–324

Barako DG, Hancock P, Izan HY (2006) Factors Influencing voluntary corporate disclosure by Kenyan companies. Corp Governance: An Int Rev 14(2):107–25

Barnea A, Rubin A (2010) Corporate social responsibility as a conflict between shareholders. J Bus Ethics 97(1):71–86

Bhagat S, Black B (2001) The non-correlation between board independence and long term firm performance. J Corp Law 27:231–274

Bihari SC, Pradhan S (2011) CSR and performance: the story of banks in India. J Trans Manage 16(1):20–35

Bradbury ME (1990) The incentives for voluntary audit committee formation. J Account Public Policy 9(1):19–36

Brammer S, Millington A (2006) Firm size, organizational visibility and corporate philanthropy: An empirical analysis. Bus Ethics: Euro Rev 15(1):6–18

Chen CJ, Jaggi B (2000) Association between independent non-executive directors, family control and financial disclosures in Hong Kong. J Account Public Policy 19(4):285–310

Cheng EC, Courtenay SM (2006) Board composition, regulatory regime and voluntary disclosure. Int J Accoun 41(3):262–289

Cheng CM, Jaggi BL (2000) The association between independent non executive directors, family control and financial disclosures, J Account Public Policy 19(4/5):285–310

Chung KH, Jo H (1996) The impact of security analysts' monitoring and marketing functions on the market value of firms. J Financ Quant Anal 31(04):493–512

Coles JL, Daniel ND, Naveen L (2008) Boards: does one size fit all? J Financ Econ 87(2):329–356

Cormier D, Magnan M, Velthoven B (2005) Environmental disclosure quality in large german companies: economic incentives, public pressures or institutional conditions? Euro acc rev 4(1)

Cowen S, Ferreri F, Parker LD (1987) The impact of corporate characteristics on social responsibility disclosure: a topology and frequency based analysis. Account Organ Soc 12(2):111–122

De Andrés P, Azofra V, Lopez F (2005) Corporate boards in OECD countries: size, composition, functioning and effectiveness. Corp Gov Int Rev 13(2):197–210

De Luca G, Perotti V (2011) Estimation of ordered response models with sample selection. Stata J Stata Corp LP 11(2):213–239

Dierkes M, Preston LE (1977) Corporate social accounting and reporting for the physical environment: a critical review and implementation proposal. Account Organ Soc 2(1):3–22

Demsetz H, Lehn K (1985) The structure of corporate ownership: causes and consequences. J Polit Econ 1155–1177

von Eije H, Megginson W (2008) Dividends and share repurchases in the european union. J Financ Econ 89:347–374

Eisenberg T, Sundgren S, Wells MT (1998) Larger board size and decreasing firm value in small firms. J Financ Econ 48(1):35–54

Eng LL, Mak YT (2003) Corporate governance and voluntary disclosure. J Account Pub Pol 22(4):325–345

Fama EF, French KR (2001) Disappearing dividends: changing firm characteristics or lower propensity to pay? J Financ Econ 60:3–44

Friedman M (1970) The social responsibility of business is to increase profits. NY Times Mag 32–33, 122–126, 13 Sept

Gallego I (2006) The use of economic, social and environmental indicators as a measure of sustainable development in spain. Corp Soc Resp Env Manag 13(2):78–97

García Sánchez IM, Rodríguez Domínguez L, Gallego Álvarez I (2011) Corporate governance and strategic information on the internet: a study of Spanish listed companies. Account Auditing Account J 24(4):471–501

Gompers P, Ishii J, Metrick A (2003) Corporate governance and equity prices. Quart J Econ 118:107–155

Goss A, Roberts GS (2011) The impact of corporate social responsibility on the cost of bank loans. J Bank Financ 35(7):1794–1810

Gul FA, Leung S (2004) Board leadership, outside directors' expertise and voluntary disclosures, J Account Public Policy 23(5):351–379

Hackston D, Milne MJ (1996) Some determinants of social and environmental isclosures in New Zealand companies. Account Audit Accoun J 9(1):77–108

Haley UCV (1991) Corporate contributions as managerial masques: reframing corporate contributions as strategies to influence society. J Manag Stud 28:485–509

Haniffa RM, Cooke TE (2005) The impact of culture and governance on corporate social reporting. J Account Public Policy 24(5):391–430

Harford J, Mansi SA, Maxwell WF (2008) Corporate governance and firm cash holdings in the US. J Financ Econ 87:535–555

Heckman JJ (1978) Dummy endogenous variables in a simultaneous equation system. Econometrica, 46(4):931–959

Heckman J (1979) Sample selection bias as a specification error. Econometrica 47:153–161

Hermalin BE, Weisbach MS (1991). The effects of board composition and direct incentives on firm performance. Financ Manage 101–112

Ho SSM, Wong KS (2001) A study of corporate disclosure practices and effectiveness in Hong Kong. J Int Financ Manag Account 12(1):75–101

Hossain M, Reaz M (2007) The determinants and characteristics of voluntary disclosure by Indian banking companies. Corp Soc Resp Env manag 14(5):274–288

Huafang X, Jianguo Y (2007) Ownership structure, board composition and corporate voluntary disclosure: Evidence from listed companies in China. Manag Audit J 22(6):604–619

Ibrahim NA, Angelidis JP (1995) The corporate social responsiveness orientation of board members: are there differences between inside and outside directors? J Bus Ethics 14(5):405–410

Jensen MC (1986) Agency cost of free cash flow, corporate finance, and takeovers. Corporate Finance, and Takeovers. Am Econ Rev 76(2)

Jensen MC (1993) The modern industrial revolution, exit, and the failure of internal control systems. the. J Finance 48(3):831–880

Jensen MC (2001) Value maximization, stakeholder theory, and the corporate objective function. J Appl Corp Finance 14(3):8–21

Jensen M, Meckling W (1976) Theory of the firm: managerial behavior, agency costs, and ownership structure. J Financ Econ 3:305–360

Jiraporn P, Chintrakarn P (2013) Corporate social responsibility (CSR) and CEO luck: are lucky CEOs socially responsible? Appl Econ Lett Taylor & Francis J 20(11):1036–1039

Jo H, Kim Y (2008) Ethics and disclosure: a study of the financial performance of firms in the seasoned equity offerings market. J Bus Ethics 80(4):855–878

Jose PD, Saraf S (2013) Corporate sustainability initiatives reporting: a study of India's most valuable companies. IIM Bangalore Research Paper, vol 428

Karamanou I, Vafeas N (2005) The association between corporate boards, audit committees, and management earnings forecasts: an empirical analysis. J Account Res 43(3):453–486

Kansal M, Joshi M, Batra GS (2014) Advances in accounting, incorporating advances in international accounting 30:217–229
Khan AF, Atkinson A (1987) Managerial attitudes to social responsibility: a comparative study in India and Britain. J Bus Ethics 6(6):419–432
Knyazeva D (2007) Corporate governance, analyst following, and firm behavior. Working Paper, SSRN.com
Lenway SA, Rehbein KA (1991) Leaders, followers, and free riders: An empirical test of the variation of corporate political involvement. Acad Manag J 34(4):1073–1090
Li H, Meng L, Wang Q, Zhou LA (2008) Political connections, financing and firm performance: evidence from chinese private firms. J Development Econ 87(2):283–299
Lim S, Matolcsy Z, Chow D (2007) The association between board composition and different types of voluntary disclosure. Eur Account Rev 16(3):555–583
Lima Crisóstomo V, de Souza Freire F, Cortes de Vasconcellos F (2011) Corporate social responsibility, firm value and financial performance in Brazil, Soc Responsib J 7(2):295–309
McGuire JB, Sundgren A, Schneeweis T (1988) Corporate social responsibility and firm financial performance. Acad Manag J 31:854–872
Meznar MB, Nigh D, Kwok CCY (1994) Effect of announcements of withdrawal from South Africa on stockholder wealth. Acad Manag Rev 37(6):1633–1648
Mishra S, Suar D (2010) Does corporate social responsibility influence firm performance of Indian companies? J Bus Ethics 95(4):571–601
Nash DR (2012) CSR: Contributions of "Maharatna" Companies of India. Asian J Res Bus Econ Manage 2(4):105–112
Navarro P (1988) Why do corporations give to charity? J Bus 61:65–93
Oana B (2010) Tata: leadership with trust, richard ivey school of business case collection. London
O'Neill HM, Saunders CB, McCarthy AD (1989) Board members, corporate social responsiveness and profitability: are tradeoffs necessary? J Bus Ethics 8(5):353–357
Pant M, Pattanayak M (2007) Insider ownership and firm value: Evidence from Indian corporate sector. Economic and Political Weekly. Accessed 21 April 2007
Pagano M, Volpin PF (2005) The political economy of corporate governance. Am Econ Rev 1005–1030
Patelli L, Prencipe A (2007) The relationship between voluntary disclosure and independent directors in the presence of a dominant shareholder. Euro Account Rev 16(1):5–33
Patten DM (1991) Exposure, legitimacy, and social disclosure. J Account Public Policy 10(4):297–308
Prado-Lorenzo JM, Gallego-Alvarez I, Garcia-Sanchez IM (2009) Stakeholder engagement and corporate social responsibility reporting: the ownership structure effect. Corp Soc Responsib Environ Manage 16(2):94–107
Ramendra S, Agarwal S (2013) Does CSR orientation reflect stakeholder relationship marketing orientation? an empirical examination of indian banks. Market Intell Plann 31(4):405–420
Roberts RW (1992) Determinants of corporate social responsibility disclosure: an application of stakeholder theory. Account Organ Soc 17(6):595–612
Rodriguez-Dominguez L, Gallego-Alvarez I, Garcia-Sanchez IM (2009) Corporate governance and codes of ethics. J Bus Ethics 90(2):187–202
Sarkar J, Sarkar S (2008) Debt and corporate governance in emerging economies Evidence from India1. Econ Transit 16(2):293–334
Scherer AG, Palazzo G, Baumann D (2006) Global rules and private actors: toward a new role of the transnational corporation in global governance. Bus Ethics Quart 16(4):505–532
Selarka E (2005) Ownership concentration and firm value: a study from the indian corporate sector. Emerg Mark Financ Tr 41(6):83–108
Sharma N (2011) CSR practices and CSR reporting in Indian banking sector. Int J Adv Econ Bus Manage 1(2):58–66

Sharma E, Mani M (2013). Corporate social responsibility: an analysis of Indian commercial banks. AIMA J Manage Res 7(1/4):0974–497
Shleifer A, Vishny RW (1986). Large shareholders and corporate control. J Polit Econ 461–488
Siegfried JJ, McElroy KM, Biernot-Fawkes D (1983) The management of corporate contributions. Res Corp Perform Policy 5:87–102
Siregar S, Bachtiar Y (2010) Corporate social reporting: empirical evidence from Indonesia Stock Exchange. Int J Islam Middle E Finance Manag 3(3):241–252
Surroca J, Tribó JA (2008) Managerial entrenchment and corporate social performance. J Bus Finance Account 35(5–6):748–789
Tirole J (2001) Corporate governance. Econometrica 69:1–38
Ullmann A (1985) Data in search of a theory: a critical examination of therelationships among social performance, social disclosure and economic performance of US firms. Acad Manag Rev 10(3):540–557
Waddock SA, Gravess SB (1997) Finding the link between stakeholder relations and quality of management. J invest 6(4):20–24
Weisbach MS (1988) Outside directors and CEO turnover. J Financ Econ 20:431–460
Willekens M, Bauwhede HV, Gaeremynck A, Van De Gucht L (2005) Internal and external governance and the voluntary disclosure of financial and non financial performance. In: 15th national BAA auditing SIG conference, pp 1–31
Yermack D (1996) Higher market valuation of companies with a small board of directors. J Financ Econ 40(2):185–211
Yu FF (2008) Analyst coverage and earnings management. J Financ Econ 88(2):245–271
Zahra SA, Stanton WW (1988) The implications of board of directors' composition for corporate strategy and performance. Int J Manage 5(2):229–236

Chapter 8
Impact of Corporate Governance on Corporate Social Responsibility: An Empirical Exploration Using Structural Equation Technique

8.1 Introduction

In the previous chapter, we have analyzed the determinants of CSR spending and activities of top 500 Indian companies focusing specifically on the impact of firm-level corporate governance structures and mechanisms on such spending. After accounting for the sample selection bias, we examine three hypotheses namely—strategic choice, over-investment and external blockholder—pertaining to the impact of nature of corporate governance at the firm level. Although we have successfully identified certain important determinants of CSR such as size, dividend payout, insider control, external blockholder and insiders' presence on the board, our results only finds a limited support towards conventional corporate governance measures such as board size and also for an alternative proxy for the insiders control on board (Duality1).

Specifically, our results provide limited explanation with respect to Duality as both the strategic choice and over-investment hypotheses imply the positive effect on CSR irrespective of whether the management is entrenched or not. Company insiders can divert resources towards socially responsible activities, because they derive private benefits from being associated with a socially responsible company (entrenchment). This implies that socially responsible behavior may only reflect the agency problem rather than the positive outcome for the shareholders where controlling managers use good relations with the stakeholders as an entrenchment strategy. In this scenario, we are more likely to observe that firms with higher insider representation on board will be associated with higher CSR spending which might further get accentuated with poor corporate governance. Though our earlier specification control for certain endogeneity in the CSR spending arising out of sample selection bias, we cannot explicitly model the interaction between the poor corporate governance and entrenchment on CSR activities.

Further, our findings might have suffered from the fact that both this attributes of corporate governance and entrenchment are unobservable and at best be captured with certain measurement errors. The conventional approach has been to include all possible corporate governance indicators in the model specification or

S.N. Bhaduri and E. Selarka, *Corporate Governance and Corporate Social Responsibility of Indian Companies*, CSR, Sustainability, Ethics & Governance,
DOI 10.1007/978-981-10-0925-9_8

to construct an Index which includes a yes/no approach to capture poor or good corporate governance.[1] In either case the approach suffers from multicollinearity as well as measurement errors.

We address this issue of unobservability and potential measurement errors as well as the correlations across all these unobservable factors measuring quality of corporate governance and entrenchment by developing an appropriate Structural Equation Model.

The most of the extant literature explaining the relationship between the CSR and corporate governance has adopted a regression framework wherein various proxies have been used for the unobservable theoretical attributes. As highlighted by Titman and Wessels (1998), the approach suffers from a number of problems. First, there may be no unique representation of the attributes we wish to measure. There are often many possible proxies for a particular attribute, and researchers, lacking theoretical guidelines, may be tempted to select those variables that work best in terms of statistical goodness-of-fit criteria, thereby biasing their interpretation of the significance levels of their tests. Second, it is often difficult to find measures of particular attributes that are unrelated to other attributes that are of interest. Thus, selected proxy variables may be measuring the effects of several different attributes. Third, since the observed variables are imperfect representations of the attributes they are supposed to measure, their use in regression analysis introduces an errors-in-variable problem. Finally, measurement errors in the proxy variables may be correlated with measurement errors in the dependent variables, creating spurious correlations even when the unobserved attribute being measured is unrelated to the dependent variable.

This chapter is organised as follows. Next section presents our empirical framework along with a brief introduction about the Structural Equation Technique and its usefulness in tracing the unobserved effects of the exogenous variables. Section 8.3, presents the model specification and estimation. Section 8.4 presents the results and Sect. 8.5 concludes.

8.2 Structural Equation Modelling

The Structural Equation Models are a combination of a "measurement model" that defines latent variables using one or more observed variables, and a "structural regression model" that links latent variables together (Kaplan 2007; Kline 2011). The parts of a structural equation model are linked to one another using a system of simultaneous regression equations. SEM is also used in the sciences, (Gillespie and Perron 2007), business, Markus (2007) education, Shelley 2007 and many other fields. Scholars (e.g., Cliff 1983; Freedman 1987; Hancock 2003)

[1]For example, based on takeover provisions, Gompers et al. (2003) construct an index of shareholder rights (GINDEX), which is a potential proxy for the extent to which a company suffers from managerial or director entrenchment.

have suggested the appropriate use of Structural Equation Model methodology in applied multivariate analysis for theory testing and causal modelling.

In the measurement model, unobservable firm-specific attributes are measured by relating them to observable variables. The measurement model can be specified as follows:

$$x = \nu + \wedge \xi + \delta,$$

Note that x is a $q \times 1$ vector of observable indicators, ξ is an $m \times 1$ vector of unobservable attributes, and $\wedge$ is a q x m matrix of regression coefficients. Errors of measurement are represented by the vector δ. In our model, we have eleven indicator variables for four attributes. Therefore, the dimensions are as follows: x is 11×1 and $\wedge$ is 11×4.

The structural model can be specified as the following system of equations:

$$\mathrm{y} = \alpha + \Gamma \xi + \varepsilon,$$

where y is a $\mathrm{p} \times 1$ vector of CSRD, Γ is a $\mathrm{p} \times \mathrm{m}$ matrix of factor loadings, and ε is a $\mathrm{p} \times 1$ vector of disturbance terms.

8.3 Model Specification

The schematic representation of our model is depicted in Fig. 8.1. Our dependent variable for the structural equation model is a categorical variable CSRD.

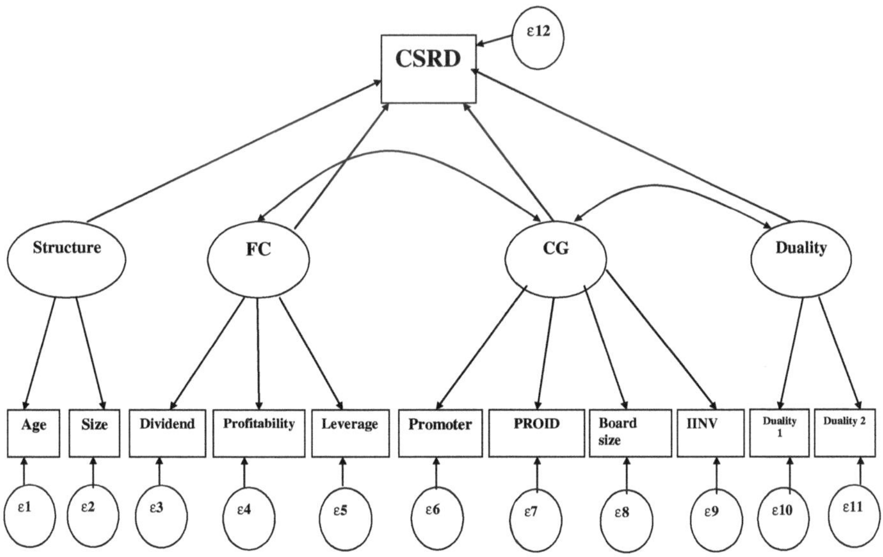

Fig. 8.1 Path diagram of SEM model specification

The proposed structural model simply states that, although the firm-specific theoretical attributes such as structure, financial constraint (FC), corporate governance (CG) and duality that supposedly determine the CSR spending cannot be observed, a number of other variables denoted as indicators such as age, size, leverage etc, that are imperfect measures of these attributes, are observable. These indicator variables can be expressed as linear functions of one or more of the unobservable attributes and a random measurement error.

Please note we include the duality separately in the model to capture the differential impact of strategic choice and entrenchment hypotheses.

Several proxies from the existing literature have been used to represent our four unobservable factors as follows. Specifically, the attribute relating to structure is measured in terms of natural log of age and total assets respectively. The attribute financial constraint is measured in terms of profitability, leverage and dividend payout respectively. The attribute corporate governance is measured in terms of promoter ownership (PROM), fraction of independent directors (PROID), board size and institutional ownership (IINV) respectively. The attribute duality is measured in terms of duality 1 and duality 2 as defined in earlier chapter.

The principal advantage of this estimation procedure over standard regression models is that it explicitly specifies the relation between the unobservable attributes and the observable variables. However, in order to identify the estimated equations, additional structure must be added. Secondly, the model allows for correlations among the unobservable attributes (the matrix Ψ) estimated within the model. This is one of the important requirements of our analysis as explained earlier.

8.3.1 Estimation

Dependent variables $x_i = (x_{i1}, \ldots, x_{ip})$ in each firm i considered manifestations of latent variables $\xi_i = (\xi_{i1}, \ldots, \xi_{im})$ with measurement error $\delta_i = (\delta_{i1}, \ldots, \delta_{ip})$ $(i = 1, \ldots, n)$.

$$\begin{aligned} x_{i1} &= \nu_1 + \lambda_{11} + \cdots + \lambda_{1m} \cdot \xi_{im} + \delta_{i1} \\ &\quad \cdot \quad\;\; \cdot \quad\;\; \cdot \quad\;\; \cdot \quad\;\; \cdot \\ &\quad \cdot \quad\;\; \cdot \quad\;\; \cdot \quad\;\; \cdot \quad\;\; \cdot \\ x_{ip} &= \nu_{\mathrm{p}} + \lambda_{1\mathrm{p}} + \cdots + \lambda_{\mathrm{p}m} \cdot \xi_{im} + \delta_{i\mathrm{p}} \end{aligned}$$

In matrix form: $x_i = \nu + \Lambda\xi_i + \delta_i$ where $\delta_i \sim N(0, \Omega)$

Linear relations between latent variables $\xi_i = (\xi_{i1}, \ldots, \xi_{im})$ and independent variables $y_i = (y_{i1}, \ldots, y_{iq})$ with residuals $\varepsilon_i = (\varepsilon_{i1}, \ldots, \varepsilon_{im})$ is specified as:

$$\begin{aligned} \xi_{i1} &= \alpha_1 + \Sigma_{j \neq 1} \beta_{1j} \xi_{ij} + \Sigma_j \pi_{1j} x_{ij} + \varepsilon_{i1} \\ &\quad \cdot \quad\;\; \cdot \quad\;\; \cdot \quad\;\; \cdot \quad\;\; \cdot \\ &\quad \cdot \quad\;\; \cdot \quad\;\; \cdot \quad\;\; \cdot \quad\;\; \cdot \\ \xi_{im} &= \alpha_m + \Sigma_{j \neq m} \beta_{mj} \xi_{ij} + \Sigma_j \pi_{mj} x_{ij} + \varepsilon_{im} \end{aligned}$$

In matrix form: $\xi_i = \alpha + B_{\xi i} + \Gamma x_i + \varepsilon_i$ where $\varepsilon_i \sim N(0, \Psi)$

$x_i|y_i \sim N\{\mu(\theta) + \prod(\theta)y_i, \sum(\theta)\}$, with $\theta = (\nu, \Lambda, \Omega, \alpha, B, \Gamma, \Psi)$

$$\mu(\theta) = \nu + \Lambda(I - B)^{-1}\alpha$$
$$\prod(\theta) = \Lambda(I - B)^{-1}\Gamma$$
$$\sum(\theta) = \Lambda(I - B)^{-1}\Psi(I - B)^{-1}\Lambda_t + \Omega$$

$$L(x, y, \theta) = \prod_{i=1}^{n} \exp\left\{-[x_i - \mu(\theta) - \prod(\theta)y_i]\sum(\theta)^{-1}[x_i - \mu(\theta) - \prod(\theta)y_i]/2\right\} \Big/ \sqrt{\left|\sum(\theta)\right|}$$

ML estimator maximizes L(x, y, θ) as a function of θ.

The maximum likelihood estimator $\widehat{\theta}$ maximizes the likelihood function as a function of θ. i.e., each parameter assigns a probability to the data we have observed. We pick the parameter value which makes our data most likely.

8.4 Results and Discussion

Table 8.1 shows the results of estimation of both structural model (Panel A) and the measurement model (Panel B). First we verify if our latent constructs built from corporate finance and corporate governance theory are validated by verifying the structural model. As reported in Panel A, we find that all the unobservable factors—structure, financial constraint, corporate governance and duality—significantly and positively affect the CSR spending.

To check for the validity of each of these unobservable factors, we refer to the measurement model estimated in Panel A. The coefficients obtained in the measurement model indicate factor loadings to explain the underlying latent construct. As hypothesized earlier, the Structure attribute is captured through significant positive loadings on age and size, is positively influencing the extent of CSR activities. Positive and significant loadings on age and size indicate that older and larger firms have better firm structure. Further, positive and significant coefficient on Structure in the structural equation indicates that firms with better structure have higher propensity to spend on CSR related activities.

Similarly, positive and significant loadings on dividend, profitability and negative and significant loading on leverage suggests that this factor captures the lack of Financial Constraint faced by the firms. This perfectly follows from the corporate finance theory which implies the firms with higher dividend payout, higher profitability and lower leverage are less constrained. As expected, the positive association between this factor and CSRD (indicated by positive and significant coefficient in the structural model) confirms our intuition that the firms facing less financial constraints are likely to engage more in CSR related activities. This is in contrast to our earlier findings that were counter intuitive in terms of

Table 8.1 Results of the structural equation estimates

	Coefficient	Std. Err.	Z	P > |z|
Panel A: structural model				
CSRD ←				
Structure	1.354	0.326	4.150	0.000
Financial constraint	1.000	(constrained)		
Corporate governance	−0.406	0.131	−3.100	0.002
Duality	0.142	0.074	1.910	0.056
Constant	1.924	0.026	74.120	0.000
Panel B: measurement model/s				
Age ←				
Structure	1	(constrained)		
Constant	3.392	0.023	145.380	0.000
Size ←				
Structure	1.470	0.414	3.550	0.000
Constant	3.639	0.022	166.620	0.000
Dividend ←				
Financial constraint	0.733	0.262	2.800	0.005
Constant	0.741	0.014	53.260	0.000
Profitability ←				
Financial constraint	0.490	0.175	2.790	0.005
Constant	0.144	0.003	48.860	0.000
Leverage ←				
Financial constraint	−0.817	0.253	−3.230	0.001
Constant	0.237	0.007	35.000	0.000
Promoter control ←				
Corporate governance	1.000	(constrained)		
Constant	0.320	0.015	21.590	0.000
Fraction of independent directors ←				
Corporate governance	−0.128	0.037	−3.460	0.001
Constant	0.545	0.008	72.030	0.000
Institutional investors ownership ←				
Corporate governance	−63.198	16.375	−3.860	0.000
Constant	21.813	0.456	47.820	0.000
Board size ←				
Corporate governance	−0.436	0.089	−4.880	0.000
Constant	2.122	0.019	110.650	0.000
Duality 1 ←				
Duality	1.000	(constrained)		
Constant	0.344	0.015	22.800	0.000
Duality 2 ←				
Duality	1.179	0.221	5.340	0.000
Constant	0.465	0.016	29.350	0.000
cov(FC,CG)	−0.002	0.001	−1.250	0.210
cov(CG, duality)	0.011	0.005	2.380	0.017

profitability and leverage (dropped because of insignificance) which did not allow us to account for the correlations among these proxies.

Next, referring to the measurement model for corporate governance factors, consistent with the literature loads up positively with promoter shareholding (captures ownership concentration more than 60 %), negatively with fraction of independent directors, board size and institutional investors' control respectively. The negative sign on fraction of independent directors, board size and institutional investors' ownership indicates lack of good corporate governance. This is because higher proportion of independent directors and institutional investor control ensures the outside control which indicates "good" governance per se. Similarly, positive loading on ownership concentration held in the hands of promoters who are in control of the management supports the entrenchment hypothesis which further justifies the lack of governance. Lack of governance that follows from the entrenchment hypothesis in the concentrated ownership set up is built on controlling shareholders' incentives to extract private benefits of control. Therefore, given the pattern of loadings, we interpret that the corporate governance factor as the poor quality of corporate governance. Note while some of the conventional corporate governance proxies such as board size and board independence have no influence in earlier analysis, now turns out to be significant drivers of CSRD.

As hypothesized, the Duality factor is positively loaded to both our empirical proxies, Duality1 and Duality2. Positive and significant loadings indicate that these two proxies capture the Duality in our sample boards which is not only indicated as type I duality (i.e. Chairman and Managing Director is the same person) but also as type II duality i.e. promoter is also Chairman of the board. Furthermore, the positive significant correlation between the Corporate Governance factor and Duality vindicates our hypothesis that these factors are likely to be correlated in reality which was not captured in earlier exercise. To summarize, our findings confirm that the extent of CSR spending is governed by factors such as Structure, Financial Constraint, and quality of corporate governance.

Formal statistical tests and fit indicates that our structural equation model moderately fits the data. Various Goodness of Fit measures for the model such as, the root mean squared error of approximation (RMSEA) of 0.10, the structural root mean square residual (SRMR) less than 0.09 and coefficient of determination as 0.99 suggest a reasonable fit of our model.

8.5 CSR and Excess Returns

In this section, we augment the structural equation model developed in the previous section to analyse the investors' assessment to the firms' decision of spending on social responsible activities. This exercise provides us a platform to understand whether shareholder value maximisation theory dominates to assess the effects of CSR allocation. Shareholder value maximisation theory predicts that firm's decision to allocate resources towards socially responsible activities after the profit is being maximized, such firms will still be able to generate higher market value. One may use Tobin's Q as a proxy for market valuation. However, Tobin's Q also indicate growth opportunities which is already internalized in the profitability. A better proxy of the effectiveness of CSR activities in improving the future valuation of the company and consequent increase in its stock price is the excess return of the company's stock over and above the market. Positive and significant excess returns indicate that investors value firms with CSR activities better than their counterparts which have not committed to CSR related activities. Our Null hypothesis follows from shareholder value maximization that commitment to undertake CSR related activities will be associated with positive excess returns. The alternate hypothesis would be either no support for shareholder value maximisation or investors' negative valuation of firms which are committed to CSR.

Excess returns are computed for each firm as:

$$Excess\_return_{i,t} = R_{i,t} - [R_f + \beta(R_{m,t} - R_f)]$$

where $R_{i,t}$, $R_{m,t}$ are the annual returns on the stock i and the BSE SENSEX for year t respectively; R_f is the risk-free rate of return and β is stock beta for each firm in year t.

Figure 8.2 describes the modified structural equation model. We test for the effects of CSRD on excess return after controlling for the unobservable factors—Structure, Financial Constraint, Corporate Governance and Duality.

Table 8.2 describes the estimation results. There are two structural models—first one is specified for CSRD and the second one is specified for Excess Returns. Positive and significant coefficients for Structure and Duality with respect to the structural model for CSRD support our earlier findings.

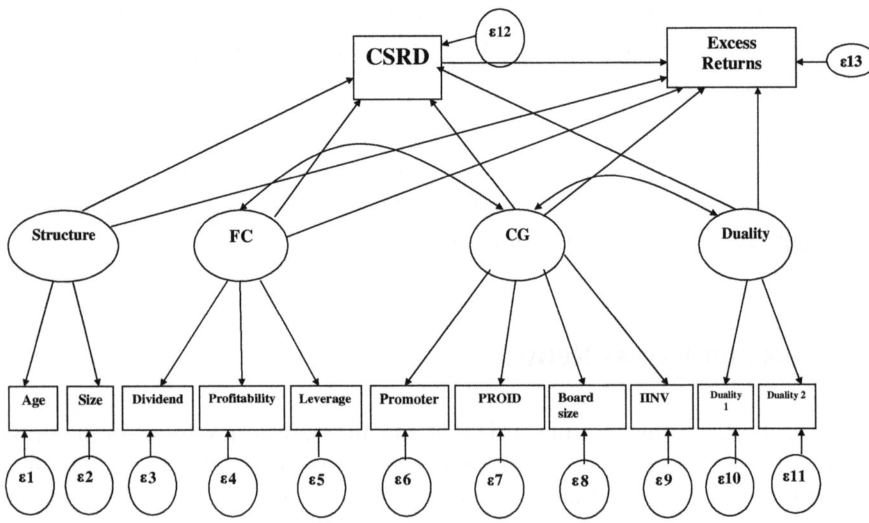

Fig. 8.2 SEM model specification—CSRD and excess returns

Table 8.2 Results of the structural equation estimates—effect of CSR on excess return

	Coefficient	Std. Err.	Z	P > |z|
Panel A: structural model				
CSRD ←				
Structure	1.396	0.334	4.18	0.000
Financial constraint	1	(constrained)		
Corporate governance	−6.410	10.965	−0.58	0.559
Duality	0.132	0.075	1.77	0.077
Constant	1.924	0.026	74.02	0.000
Excess Return ←				
CSRD	0.001	0.035	0.02	0.980
Structure	−0.287	0.231	−1.25	0.213
Financial constraint	1.064	0.425	2.50	0.012
Corporate governance	1	(constrained)		
Duality	−0.040	0.058	−0.70	0.486
Constant	0.224	0.071	3.15	0.002
Panel B: measurement model/s				
Age ←				
Structure	1	(constrained)		
Constant	3.391	0.023	145.15	0.000
Size ←				
Structure	1.693	0.549	3.08	0.002
Constant	3.634	0.022	166.67	0.000
Dividend ←				
Financial constraint	0.708	0.256	2.76	0.006
Constant	0.740	0.014	53.14	0.000
Profitability ←				
Financial constraint	0.608	0.241	2.52	0.012
Constant	0.144	0.003	48.88	0.000
Leverage ←				
Financial constraint	−0.781	0.241	−3.23	0.001
Constant	0.237	0.007	34.97	0.000
Promoter control ←				
Corporate governance	16.312	27.319	0.60	0.550
Constant	0.320	0.015	21.60	0.000
Fraction of independent directors ←				
Corporate governance	−2.095	3.532	−0.59	0.553
Constant	0.545	0.008	71.94	0.000
Institutional investors ownership ←				
Corporate governance	−985.065	1692.277	−0.58	0.561
Constant	21.828	0.457	47.82	0.000
Board size ←				
Corporate governance	−7.128	12.023	−0.59	0.553
Constant	2.121	0.019	110.43	0.000

(continued)

Table 8.2 (continued)

	Coefficient	Std. Err.	Z	P > lzl
Duality 1←				
Duality	1	(constrained)		
Constant	0.343	0.015	22.76	0.000
Duality 2 ←				
Duality	1.136	0.210	5.40	0.000
Constant	0.463	0.016	29.25	0.000
cov(FC,CG)	−0.000	0.000	−0.52	0.605
cov(CG, duality)	0.001	0.001	0.57	0.567

The coefficient of CSRD in the structural model specifying excess return is insignificant. This means that future valuation of company does not depend on its decision to undertake CSR activities. This implies that investors are indifferent with the CSR related expenses. In fact, only financial constraint factor explains the variation in the excess return of firms which is in line with the corporate finance theories built on profitability, leverage and dividend payout policies. Furthermore, the positive and significant loadings on profitability and dividend payout along with the negative and significant loading on the leverage indicate that the financial constraint factor captures the lack of financial constraint faced by the firm. Overall our finding is perfectly in line with the theory that firms which face less financial constraint are valued better by the investors.

Overall, our results support the role of corporate governance in CSR propensity but the later does not affect the market valuation of sample firms.

8.6 Conclusion

This chapter presents the structural equation model that address two critical issues related to the unobservability of the attributes derived from various theoretical constructs and potential measurement errors. Further the proposed model also incorporates the possibility of cross-correlations across the unobservable factors.

The results show that all the four specified attributes—Structure, Financial Constraint, Corporate Governance and Duality—significantly influence the CSR spending of large Indian firms. More specifically, we find evidence that poor corporate governance coupled with insider control over the board tend to explain the variation in CSR activities across firms. The other conventional factors such as age, size and financial viability of a firm also contribute to the CSR spending by these firms.

References

Cliff N (1983) Some cautions concerning the application of casual modeling methods. Multivar Behav Res 18:115–126

Freedman DA (1987) As others see us: a case study in path analysis. J Educ Behav Stat 12(2):101–128

Gillespie D, Perron B (2007) Structural equation modeling. In: Boslaugh S (ed) Encyclopedia of epidemiology. Sage, pp 1005–1009

Gompers P, Ishii J , Metrick A (2003) Corporate governance and equity prices. Q J Econ 118:107–55

Hancock, Greogry R (2003) Fortune Cookies, Measurement Error, And Experimental Design, J Mod Appl Stat Methods 2 (2):293–305

Kaplan SN (2007) Are CEOs really overpaid? Corporate Board 28(167):8–12

Kline RB (2011) Principles and practice of structural equation modeling, 3rd ed. New York: The rd Guilford Press

Markus K (2007) Structural equation modeling. In Rogelberg, Steve. Encyclopedia of Industrial and Organizational Psychology. Sage:774–777

Shelley M (2007) Structural equation modeling. In: English FW (ed) Encyclopedia of educational leadership and administration. Sage

Titman S, Wessels R (1988) The determinants of capital structure choice. J Financ 43(1):1–19

Appendix

Definitions of Corporate Social Responsibility

Author (year)	Proposed construct	Definition
Bowen (1953)	Businessmen social responsibility	"It refers to the obligations of businessmen to pursue those policies, to make those decisions, or to follow those lines of actions which are desirable in terms of the objectives and values of our society" (p. 6)
Davis (1960)	Corporate social responsibility	"Businessmen's decisions and actions taken for reasons at least partially beyond the firm's direct economic or technical interest" (p. 70)
McGuire (1963)	Corporate social responsibility	"The idea of social responsibilities supposes that the corporation has not only economic and legal obligations but also certain responsibilities to society which extend beyond these obligations" (p. 144)
Walton (1967)	Corporate social responsibility	"In short, the new concept of social responsibility recognizes the intimacy of the relationships between the corporation and society and realizes that such relationships must be kept in mind by top managers as the corporation and the related groups pursue their respective goals" (p. 18)

(continued)

S.N. Bhaduri and E. Selarka, *Corporate Governance and Corporate Social Responsibility of Indian Companies*, CSR, Sustainability, Ethics & Governance,
DOI 10.1007/978-981-10-0925-9

(continued)

Author (year)	Proposed construct	Definition
Maignan and Ferrell (2000)	Corporate citizenship	"The extent to which businesses meet the economic, legal, ethical and discretionary responsibilities imposed on them by their stakeholders" (p. 284)
McWilliams and Siegel (2001)	Corporate social responsibility	"Here, we define CSR as actions that appear to further some social good, beyond the interest of the firm and that which is required by law" (p. 117)
Baker (2003)	Business process	CSR is about how companies manage the business processes to produce an overall positive impact on society
Matten and Crane (2005)	Corporate citizenship	"Corporate citizenship describes the role of the corporation in administering citizenship rights for individuals" (p. 173)
Campbell (2006)	Corporate social responsibility	"I view corporations as acting in socially responsible ways if they do two things. First, they must not knowingly do anything that could harm their stakeholders. Second, if they do harm to stakeholders, then they must rectify it whenever it is discovered and brought to their attention" (p. 928)
Crouch (2006)	Corporate social responsibility	"…behaviour by firms that voluntarily takes account of the externalities produced by their market behaviour, externalities being defined as results of market transactions that are not themselves embodied in such transactions. CSR is essentially corporate externality recognition" (p. 1534)
Basu and Palazzo (2008)	Corporate social responsibility	"…we can define CSR as the process by which managers within an organization think about and discuss relationships with stakeholders as well as their roles in relation to the common good, along with their behavioral disposition with respect to the fulfilment and achievement of these roles and relationships." (p. 124)

International Organisations on Corporate Social Responsibility

Organisation	Definition
World Business Council for Sustainable Development (WBCSD) (2003)	Corporate Social Responsibility is business' commitment to contribute to sustainable economic development working with employees, their families, the local community, and society at large to improve their quality of life
CSR Europe (2003)	Corporate Social Responsibility is the way in which a company manages and improves its social and environmental impact to generate value for both its shareholders and its stakeholders by innovating its strategy, organisation and operations
Organisation for Economic Co-operation and Development (OECD) (2003)	Corporate Responsibility involves the 'fit' businesses develop with the societies in which they operate. [...] The function of business in society is to yield adequate returns to owners of capital by identifying and developing promising investment opportunities and, in the process, to provide jobs and to produce goods and services that consumers want to buy. However, corporate responsibility goes beyond this core function. Businesses are expected to obey the various laws which are applicable to them and often have to respond to societal expectations that are not written down as formal law
Amnesty International—Business Group (UK) (2002)	Companies [have] to recognise that their ability to continue to provide goods and services and to create financial wealth will depend on their acceptability to an international society which increasingly regards protection of human rights as a condition of the corporate licence to operate
The Corporate Responsibility Coalition (CORE) (2003)	As an 'organ of society', companies have a responsibility to safeguard human rights within their direct sphere of operations as well as within their wider spheres of influence
Novethic (2003)	Linked to the application by corporations of the sustainable development principle, the concept of CSR integrates three dimensions: an economic dimension (efficiency, profitability), a social dimension (social responsibility) and an environmental dimension (environmental responsibility). To respect these principles, corporations must pay more attention to all the stakeholders [...] which inform on the expectations of civil society and the business environment

(continued)

(continued)

Organisation	Definition
Unilever (2003)	We define social responsibility as the impact or interaction we have with society in three distinct areas: (i) voluntary contributions, (ii) impact of (business's direct) operations, and (iii) impact through the value chain
Novo Nordisk (2003)	Social responsibility for Novo Nordisk is about caring for people. This applies to our employees and the people whose healthcare needs we serve. It also considers the impact of our business on the global society and the local community. As such, social responsibility is more than a virtue—it is a business imperative

County Wise Focus on CSR Practices

Country	Author	Sector	CSR practice
Europe	Furrer et al. (2009)	Education	Business students attribute more importance to environmental CR and less importance to social CR than managers
Europe	Steurer (2010)	The role of governments in CSR	Characterizing public policies CSR started out as a neo-liberal concept that helped to downscale government regulations, but that it has in turn matured into a more progressive approach of societal co-regulation
Indonesia	Arli and Lasmono (2010)	Consumers' perception of CSR	Consumers are often unaware and unsupportive towards CSR. But When consumers have to buy similar products with the same price and quality, CSR could be the determining factor. Eg. ITC notebooks
Chinese	Ramasamy and Yeung (2009)	Consumers perception of CSR	Economic responsibilities are most important while philanthropic responsibilities are of least importance

(continued)

(continued)

Country	Author	Sector	CSR practice
Mexico	Muller and Kolk (2009)	Auto industry	Local companies do engage in the type of CSR activities commonly associated with CSR in developed countries
Germany and UK	Silberhorn and Warren (2007)	CSR view from big companies	German companies could benefit more from demonstrating a broad, business-driven understanding of CSR
Finland	Kapoor and Sandhu (2010)	Compares CSR practices of forest company, a cooperative bank, and a retail cooperative	The local corporate social responsibility should be in balance with global corporate social responsibility. Companies have still much work to do for good "corporation citizenship"
Japan	Fukukawa and Teramoto (2009)	Multinational companies	Japanese business is not keeping up with corporate social responsibility practices, and it needs to achieve a more global mode of transparency and accountability
United States, Europe, and Asia	Hill (2007)	Company stock market valuation	European countries and United States represented in this study are best characterized by horizontal individualism. Thus, their possible impact on socially responsible investing may be very different than Asian investors
Asia	Chapple and Moon (2005)	CSR web site reporting	Multinational companies are more likely to adopt CSR than those operating solely in their home country
India	Murthy (2008)	Top software firms	Corporate social disclosure practices of the top 16 software firms in India. Firms had different motives/reasons for reporting the different attributes of CSR

(continued)

(continued)

Country	Author	Sector	CSR practice
India	Chaudhri et al. (2007)	Information technology (IT) companies	IT companies in India are lagging behind in creative and effective CSR communication on their web sites. Multinational corporations would do well to proactively present CSR information on country specific sites as an expression of their commitment to local communities
India	Kapoor and Sandhu (2010)	Impact of corporate social responsibility on financial performance	Bi-dimensional model
India	Kiran and Sharma (2011a)	Education	Introduce CSR into course-work of management curriculum
India	Kiran and Sharma (2011b)	Health, education and environment	Investment in CSR initiatives vary according to the firm size. Need of the hour is for the development of CSR framework

Schools of Thoughts on CSR

In the literature on CSR, one can come across three schools of thoughts which has its own pros and cons. Michael, 2003 elaborate the focus and left out aspects of each schools of thought:

1. Neoliberal school
   Self-regulation by industry in accordance to the risks and rewards of CSR activities but failing to address the resource misallocations and unintended consequences by CSR.

2. The state-led school
   This school of thought focuses on the international and national regulation and cooperation but failing to address the underlying politics behind government encouraging CSR.

3. The 'third-way' school
   It focus on the roles of not-for-profit and for profit organisations but failing to address the self-interests of participating individuals involved in CSR.

Distribution of CSRD Across Sample Years

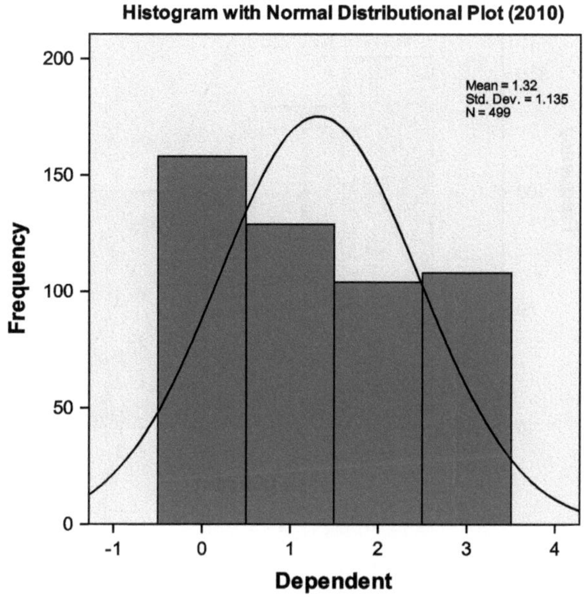

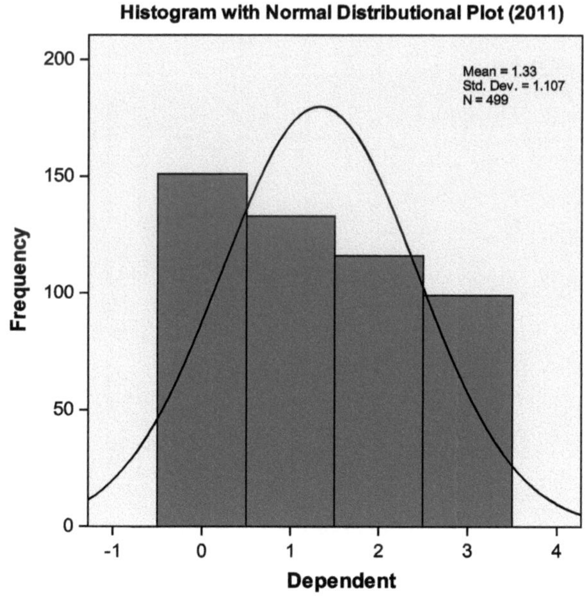

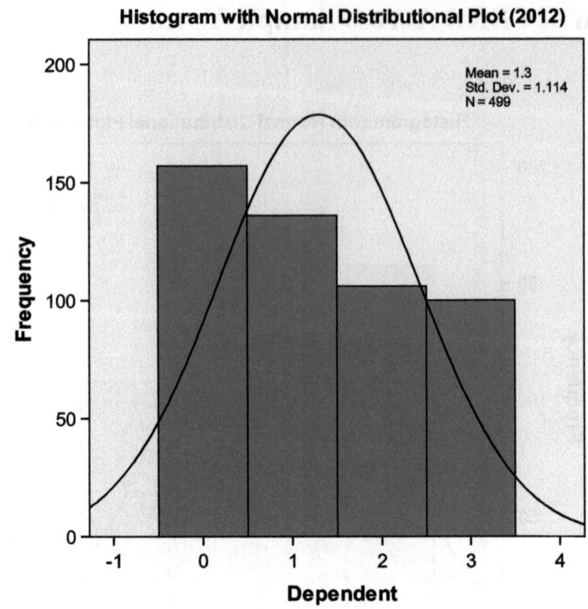
Histogram with Normal Distributional Plot (2012)
Mean = 1.3
Std. Dev. = 1.114
N = 499
Frequency
200
150
100
50
0
-1
0
1
2
3
4
Dependent

MIX
Papier aus verantwortungsvollen Quellen
Paper from responsible sources
FSC® C105338

If you have any concerns about our products,
you can contact us on
ProductSafety@springernature.com

In case Publisher is established outside the EU,
the EU authorized representative is:
Springer Nature Customer Service Center GmbH
Europaplatz 3, 69115 Heidelberg, Germany

Printed by Libri Plureos GmbH
in Hamburg, Germany